Learn Python Programming:

The Crash Course to Learn Python Language and its Application for Data Science with Python 3. A Beginner's Guide to Python Machine Learning with Practical Examples

Mark J. Branson

Table of Contents

Introduction

Congratulations on purchasing *Learn Python Programming* and thank you for doing so.

Books about the subject flood the market and we thank you for picking this one! All attempts were made to make this book has the most useful information. Enjoy!

The term "learning" encompasses a wide range of processes; if one were to look it up on the dictionary, they would come across definitions equally "to gain knowledge, or understanding of, or skill in, by study, instruction, or experience," along with "a modification of a behavioral tendency by experience." In the same way that psychologists the application with the study of humans, this text will certain on the learning processes of machines. The two spheres of animal learning and machine learning are clearly connected; a few techniques in machine learning are actually derived from some techniques used in animal learning. In addition, breakthroughs in machine learning can help bring to light a few facets of biological learning.

When it comes to machines, superficially speaking, it can be said that any change to a machine's structure, data stored in memory or composition in order to make the machine better performing and more efficient can point to the sign of learning in a machine. However, when we delve deeper, we see that only a few of these changes can be categorized as machine learning. For instance, consider a machine that is meant to predict weather forecasts in a certain area for a few weeks. If data about the weather in the area over the past year is added to the memory of the machine, the machine can learn from this data and predict the weather more accurately. This is a perfect example of machine learning.

Python is a programming language that contains all the functionality that a modern programming language should have: besides having an efficient high-level data structure, Python also has all the functional facilities to program in the paradigm of object-oriented programming. Presented that way, very crudely, the terms mentioned may not be something that beginners are familiar with.

By mentioning them, we only intend to assure the reader that when learning Python he is venturing with a modern and sophisticated programming language, which will allow him to understand without problems the structures of other modern programming languages (or that have been modernized) such as C ++ and Java.

As an additional advantage, with a simple and elegant syntax, Python combines in a single environment facilities to execute numerical, symbolic or algebraic computation and visualization that are portable (as they are developed) from one computer system to another (for example from any distribution). From Linux to another operating system where Python works).

In the course of this book, we will look at everything you need to know about Machine learning using Python. Each chapter will take you one step closer to machine learning programming using Python. Included are sample codes and case studies that will further help you test your knowledge.

Chapter 1: What is Machine Learning?

With the changing face of technology, machines with artificial intelligence have become responsible for tasks such as prediction, diagnosis, recognition, etc. These types of machines "learn" from data that is added to them. This data is called training data because it is used to train the machine. The machines analyze patterns in this data and then put these patterns to use. Machines use different learning mechanisms to analyze the data depending on the actions they are required to perform, and they can be divided into two categories - unsupervised learning and supervised learning.

People may wonder why machines are not designed specifically for the tasks that they need to carry out, but there are many reasons as to why machine learning is advantageous. As mentioned earlier, research into the field of machine learning can help us had better understand certain aspects of human learning, and machine learning can increase the accuracy and efficiency of machines.

For example, take Jack and Joy, two avid music listeners. By accessing their listening history, a music streaming Service Company can use machine learning to find out what songs they prefer by having access to their listening history. As a music company, I can use machine learning to map what kind of songs are preferred by each of them and thereby determine how to sell my product to them. For example, I could note various attributes of songs - like tempo, frequency or gender of voice and use these factors and maybe plot a graph - over a period of time, it becomes obvious that Jack tends to listen to songs that have a fast tempo and sung by a male and Joy prefers slow songs sung by a female singer etc. This can then be fed to the marketing team and drive product decisions.

Today, we have access to years of historical data dating back to the birth of technology, or to be more precise, to the first time, we had the ability to store and process such large- scale systems and data. Technology has matured to handle such operations and the pervasiveness of networks today ensures access to more data to mine from than ever before.

A few other reasons are:
Even with the greatest efforts by engineers, some tasks cannot be defined explicitly, and need to be explained to the machine using examples. The idea is to train the machine with the input and teach it how to reach the output. This way, the machine will know how to deal with future inputs and process them to reach appropriate outputs.

Machine learning is also intertwined with the field of data mining. Data mining is essentially the process of looking through vast amounts of data to find important correlations and relationships. This is another advantage of machine learning as it might lead to the finding of important information.
On many occasions, humans design machines without correctly estimating the surrounding conditions in which they will be functioning, which can play a huge role in the

performance of the machine. In such cases, machine learning can help in the acclimation of the machine to its environment in order for the performance not to be hindered. In addition, environmental changes may occur and machine learning will help the machine to adapt to these changes without missing performance.

Another loophole in the hard coding process from human beings into the machine is the fact that the process might be extremely elaborate. In such a case, the programmer might miss a few details since it would be a very tedious job to encode all the details. Therefore, it is much more desirable to allow the machine to learn such processes.

There are constant changes in the world, whether in technology, vocabulary, and in many other areas, and redesigning systems to accommodate every change is impractical. Instead, machine-learning methods can be used to train the machines to adapt to these changes.

Advantages of Machine Learning

Now that we have an understanding of what machine learning is, here are a few advantages.

- One can use machine learning to handle multi-variety and multi-dimensional data in static and dynamic environments.

- Machine learning helps to improve the efficiency of processes, thereby improving an individual' s productivity.

- You can use different machine learning tools to provide high-quality work regardless of the complexity of the process.

- There are many practical advantages for machine learning. For instance, you can develop autonomous software programs and computers. This helps to automate some tasks.

Disadvantages of Machine Learning

- One of the major problems with machine learning is the acquisition. Since the data uses different algorithms, it will first need to be processed to ensure that the algorithm produces the desired results.

- Since some machine learning algorithms have to interpret the input, the developer must find a way to determine the effectiveness of the algorithm that is sometimes difficult to do.

- The uses of machine learning algorithms are limited, and you can never be certain that an algorithm will work in every case you can think of. Therefore, before you use or apply a machine-learning algorithm, you must fully understand it, and verify that it will work for your problem.

- Machine learning algorithms, like deep learning algorithms, must be trained using a training dataset. In most cases, you have a large dataset, which is difficult to work with.

- It is also important to note that machine-learning algorithms are susceptible to errors. If the algorithm does make an error, it becomes difficult to diagnose and correct that error since you will need to go through the underlying complexities of the algorithm.

- A machine-learning algorithm does not always make a prediction immediately. You should also remember that the algorithm learns through historical data, therefore, this algorithm is not always exposed to the ongoing situation. This deteriorates the performance of the algorithm.

Now that you are aware of some of the advantages and disadvantages of machine learning, let us look at the different fields in which you can apply machine learning. You must remember that you can overcome these disadvantages using the correct training dataset.

Applications of Machine Learning

Today, machine learning is transforming the way businesses are run by operating on the vast data that is now available and drawing meaningful information and predictions out of it.

Machine Learning is now a solution to complete tasks that would be impossible to complete manually in such a short time and with such a large amount of data. In this decade, we are overcome with data and information and have no manual way of processing this information, thus paving the way for automated processes and machines to do that job for us.

Useful information can be derived when the process of analysis and discovery becomes automated, which will help us drive our future actions in an automated process. We have therefore entered the world of Business Analytics, Data Science, and Big Data. Business Intelligence and Predictive analytics are no longer just for the elite as it is now accessible to small companies and businesses. This has given these small businesses a chance to participate in the process of collecting and utilizing information effectively. Let us look at some technical uses of machine learning and how they can be applied to real-world problems.

Density Estimation

This use of machine learning allows the system to use the data provided to create a product that looks like it. For instance, if you were to pick up War and Peace from the shelves of a bookstore and run it through a machine, the machine would be able to determine the density of the words in the book and provide us with similar novels.

Latent Variables

When you work with latent variables, the machine uses the method of clustering to determine whether the variables are related to one another. This is a useful tool when you do not know what the cause of change in different variables is and when you do not know the relationship between these variables. Additionally, when the data set is large, it is better to look for latent variables as it helps to comprehend the data obtained.

Reduction of Dimensionality

Most of the time, the data obtained have different variables and dimensions. If there are more than three dimensions, it is impossible for the human mind to visualize the data. In these instances, machine learning can help in reducing the data into a manageable number of dimensions so that the user easily understands the relationship between the different variables.

Visualization

Sometimes, the user would just like to visualize the existing relationship between variables or would like to obtain a data summary in visual form. In these instances, machine learning helps by summarizing the data for the user using specified or non – specified parameters.

To summarize the main points, machine learning models train systems to learn from existing data and offer various services such as prediction and classification which have several real-life applications such as self-driving cars, phones with face recognition or devices such as Google Home and Alexa which respond to your accent with more accuracy the longer you use it.

Today machine learning and artificial intelligence are revamping the way healthcare institutions, publishing companies, weather predictors, travel fare and route predictors and several other traditional domains are run, such as healthcare, with machine learning assisting in every phase from predicting the potential health risks based on family history to a full diagnosis of ailments.

Other everyday examples of machine learning in our everyday lives include predicting stock market prices, platforms such as YouTube or Netflix recommending content based on your watch history and Gmail detecting and classifying emails into the spam folder.

Chapter 2: Machine Learning - Concepts & Terms

Machine learning is essentially the concept of training machines to do things which humans are normally good at by feeding relevant and repetitive training data sets.

An ordinary system simply processes the input data according to the written function and gives an output, whereas a system with artificial intelligence can learn, predict and even improve on its results.

Let us analyze this with a very simple example of how a child learns to identify objects.

Imagine parents introducing apples before a child, describing the apple as a red and round object and the orange as around an orange object.

 ------------------> [Apple, round, red]

-----------------> [Apple]

Here, apple and orange are "labels" and the shape "round" and color "red/orange" are attributes.

Similarly, a machine is trained with a data set of "labels" and "attributes", and then learns to identify the object based on the attribute data given as input.

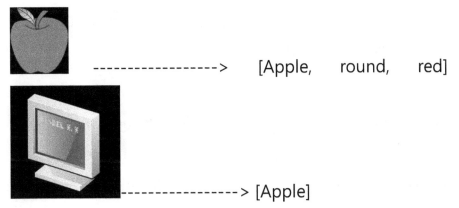 ------------------>   [Apple,   round,   red]

------------------> [Apple]

This type of classification model based on labeled data is called a supervised learning model. In the same way that humans are being supervised and taught in school, this model also provides scope for feedback.

Let us take the example of a [round, red] input. So far, the machine/child has only learned that anything that is round and red is an apple. However, the object they are now encountering is a cricket ball, so the machine can be fed feedback of -1 or 0, depending on whether the prediction is correct or false. Over a course of time, the machine may add other features such as taste and other attributes to attain more accuracy, and this is the way that machines learn. Therefore, high-quality data, larger data sets and longer training time lead to better results, just like a child who is well tutored.

Of course, this is a very simple classification model of a machine learning system. In subsequent chapters, we will learn about more complex systems and concepts that will show us how the machine differentiates a cricket ball from an apple, which both have the 'red' and 'round' attributes.

Before proceeding further, you need to know the difference between the concept of Deep Learning, Machine Learning, and Artificial Intelligence, which are often used interchangeably but do not mean the same thing.

Machine Learning, Artificial Intelligence, and Deep Learning

The following diagram shows how these terms are related – essentially, Machine Learning and Deep Learning are a subset under the umbrella of Artificial Learning.

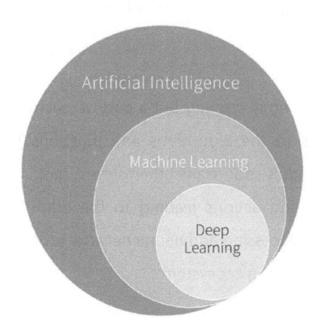

Image: An illustration to understand the relationship between Machine Learning, Artificial Intelligence, and Deep Learning.

Essentially, Artificial intelligence refers to making machines mimic human behavior with better accuracy and efficiency. Some examples include IBM' s Watson and the Deep Blue Chess, a chess-playing computer that has beat chess masters.

To be more precise, machine learning is the actual statistical, mathematical model that enables the machines to learn how to mimic human behavior based on past data.

Deep Learning is nothing but a part of machine learning and refers to the algorithms and functions that allow these models to train themselves and take the corresponding actions leading to the outputs. Natural language processing and neural network tools are part of the deep learning ecosystem.

Objectives of Machine Learning System

The machine learning systems primarily have one of the following objectives:

Predict a category

The machine-learning model that reads the input data and predicts which category the data will fall under and the prediction output is most likely to be a binary yes or no answer.

For example - will it rain, is this a fruit or a vegetable, and is the email-received spam? This is achieved by reference to a set of data which will indicate this is likely to be spam, in the email example here, based on certain keywords. This is called "Classification".

Predict a quantity

This system is typically used to predict a value; for example, predicting rainfall based on various attributes such as humidity, air pressure, etc. This kind of prediction is called "Regression", and there are further subdivisions in regression algorithms such as linear regression, multiple regressions, etc.

Anomaly Detector Systems

Of course, other machine learning systems are more domain-specific like "Anomaly detection" , where the purpose of the model is to detect any outliers in the given data. A typical application of such a model can be seen in the banking industry or in online e-commerce systems where the system is specifically built to detect any unusual transactions, as they are likely to be fraudulent and immediately report them for further investigation.

Clustering Systems

Clustering systems are still in the nascent stages, but they have the potential to drive businesses in the future. These systems are primarily used in use cases that group the users into different clusters based on certain behavioral factors; for example, if a certain age group in a particular region prefers watching a specific program. Based on this clustering, the service now suggests what program you are likely to watch and enjoy based on which cluster bucket you are more likely to belong to.

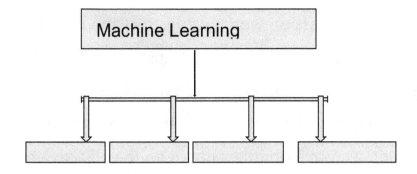

Category of Machine Learning systems:

- Supervised Learning

- Unsupervised Learning

- Reinforced Learning

Normally, in the case of classical machines, a programmer gives the machine a set of instructions and input parameters, which are then computed by the machine to get an output once the system processes the data using the specific commands. As far as machine learning goes, the system is not restricted by the commands given by the programmer - the machine picks the algorithm that can process the dataset to get the desired output based on previous historical data and experience.

Thus, in the classical world, we instruct the machines to process data according to a set of instructions, whereas in the machine learning era, we do not instruct the system per se, instead, the computers interact with the data set, develop its own algorithms based on the objective of the system, make its own decisions like a human would analyze and give an output, with the ability to process much larger data set quicker and with much higher accuracy.

There are various learning algorithms, primarily categorized based on the purpose of the algorithm, and they can be broadly classified under the following class of learning.

Supervised Learning

Supervised learning means when the system learns to make predictions based on "labeled" data. In other words, a "supervisor" determines the output of the system, and these types of algorithms are called predictive algorithms.

For example, consider the following table:

Currency (label)	Weight (Feature)
1 USD	10 gms
1 EUR	5 gm
1 INR	3 gm
1 RU	7 gm

In the table, different currency coins are given an attribute - weight. Here, the currency or coin is the label and weight is the feature.

First, a supervised system is fed this training data and subsequently, when it comes across an input of 3gm, for example, it will predict the coin is a one INR coin based on its previous learning. If the weight is detected to weigh 10gm, the machine learns to detect it as a 1-dollar coin.

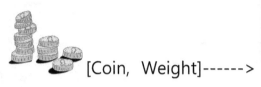 [Coin, Weight]------>  [Machine learning model-----> [Classify]

Regression and Classification algorithms fall under the category of supervised learning.

Regression systems are used to predict house prices, the outcome of sports games, etc., whereas classification systems' mission is to find which category a user belongs to.

Some of these algorithms will be discussed in detail later on, and you will learn how to implement these algorithms using a sample python code.

Unsupervised Learning

In this model, the system is a little bit more sophisticated, as it finds a pattern when working with "unlabeled data" as output. It is typically the kind of algorithm that is used to draw meaningful inference from very large data sets. This kind of model can also be called a "descriptive model" , as it uses data and summarizes it, generating a description of the different datasets. This type of model is typically used in data mining applications that involve an extremely large volume of unstructured input data.

For example, if the system is fed an input of names, runs, and wickets as input, the system visualizes the data points on a graph and learns that there are two clusters - one with more runs as batsmen and the other with more wickets as bowlers. When a new input is fed, the person is likely to fall within one of these clusters and this thereby predicts whether he is more likely to be a bowler or a batsman.

Name	Runs	Wickets
Rachel	100	3
John	10	50
Paul	60	10
Sam	250	6
Alex	90	60

Based on this the cluster model, sample data set for a match can group the players into batsmen, bowlers, etc.

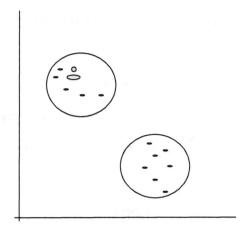

Image: Illustration of a sample graph showing how the data is plotted and clustered.

Some of the common algorithms that can be categorized under unsupervised learning include density estimation, clustering, compressing and data reduction.

Clustering algorithms that are under unsupervised learning – what they basically do is summarize the data and describe and present it a new way, a model which is mostly used in data mining applications. Density estimation is used when the objective is to visualize a large set of data and create a meaningful summary out of it, which brings us to the concept of data reduction and dimensionality, where it' s important to deliver the summary without the loss of useful information, or in other words to reduce the complexity of data while delivering useful output.

Reinforced learning

This is more akin to how humans learn, as the system learns to behave in a given environment by taking action based on a given set of data. For example, we learn not to touch fire because we are told that it hurts, or we might put our finger under a flame and learn that it hurts the hard way, and are most likely to be careful around the fire in the future. This is essentially a class of algorithm called reinforced learning.

The following table summarizes and gives an overview of the key differences between supervised and unsupervised learning. It also lists some popular algorithms used for each class of learning models.

Supervised Learning	Unsupervised Learning
Works with labeled data	Works with unlabeled data
Takes Direct feedback	No feedback loop
Predicts output based on input data Therefore, it is also called "Predictive Algorithm"	Finds the hidden structure/pattern from input data Sometimes called a "Descriptive Model"
Some common classes of supervised algorithms include: Regression, Classification Name of Algorithms Logistic Regression Linear Regression (Numeric prediction) Polynomial Regression Regression trees (Numeric prediction)	Some common classes of unsupervised algorithms include: Clustering, compressing, density estimation & data reduction Name of Algorithms K-means Clustering (Clustering) Association Rules (Pattern Detection)

Gradient Descent Random Forest Decision Trees (classification) K-Nearest Algorithm (classification) Naive Bayes Support Vector Machines	Singular Value Decomposition Fuzzy Means Partial Least Squares Apriority Hierarchical Clustering Principal Component Analysis

Table: Supervised Vs Unsupervised Learning.

We will briefly look at each of these algorithms, their implementation details and we will learn how to implement them with python in the next chapter.

We will now look at some everyday scenarios where machine learning is applied, and the reader is encouraged to guess the correct category of the machine-learning model that is being used in each of the scenarios. The answers will be given in the next section.

- Facebook face recognition algorithm

- Netflix or YouTube recommending programs based on past viewership history

- Analyzing large volumes of bank transactions to guess if they are valid or fraudulent transactions.

- Umber's surge pricing algorithm

Steps in building a Machine learning System

Irrespective of the type of machine learning model, the common steps that are typically involved in designing a Machine Learning system are the following:

Define Objective

Like any task, it is important to define the purpose of your system. What you want to predict will determine the kind of data, the algorithm you will use, and so forth.

Collect Data

When building a machine learning system, the most time-consuming step is collecting relevant data that will be used to train the algorithm.

Prepare Data

This step is often overlooked as trivial but proves costly if not taken care of. The cleaner and more relevant the data set is, the more accurate the prediction/ output is.

Select Algorithm

Various algorithms such as Structured Vector Machine (SVM), K-nearest, Naive-Bayes, and Apriority exist, so an appropriate algorithm is chosen to achieve the objective of the model.

Train Model

The data collected is fed to the system and the algorithm is trained to predict.

Test Model

Once the model is trained, it is ready to read input and generate outputs.

Predict

Multiple iterations are run and sometimes, feedback is fed to the system.

Deploy

Once a model is tested and confirmed to be working as expected, the said model is serialized and integrated into an application of choice in order to then be deployed.

These steps could vary depending on the exact application and type of algorithm, whether supervised or unsupervised, but it is a good template highlighting the steps involved in designing any machine learning system. There are multiple languages and tools used at each of these stages, and in this book, we will see how to design a few simple machine learning systems using Python. Before we go on to see each of these steps in detail, we will first learn some basics of programming using Python. The next chapter will discuss the rationale behind choosing Python, before an introduction to programming using this programming language.

The answer to the quiz in the previous section:

Scenario 1: Facebook recognizes the friend in a picture from another album including tagged photographs

Explanation: This explains supervised learning. In this case, Facebook is using tagged photos to recognize the person in question. Therefore, the tagged photos become the labels of the pictures and we know that when the machine learns from labeled data, this is supervised learning.

Scenario 2: Recommending new songs based on someone's past music choices

Explanation: This is another example of supervised learning. The model is training a classifier on pre-existing labels (genres of songs). This is what Netflix, Pandora, and Spotify do - they collect the songs/movies that you like, evaluate the features based on these likes/dislikes and then recommend new movies/songs based on similar features.

Scenario 3: Analyze bank data for suspicious-looking transactions and flag the fraud transactions

Explanation: This is an example of unsupervised learning. In this case, the suspicious transactions are not defined; hence, there are no labels for "fraud" and "not fraud". The model tries to identify outliers by looking at anomalous transactions to flag them as 'fraud' .

Scenario 4: Combination of various models

Explanation: Uber's price surge is a combination of several machine learning models, including prediction to determine peak hours and traffic in a certain area, to the availability of cabs, and clustering to determine usage patterns in different areas of the city. It uses a combination of these learning models to dynamically surge prices and to efficiently map customers to available cabs.

Univariate linear regression

Univariate linear regression a very basic supervised learning algorithm that aims to find the best possible line using a single explanatory variable (we also speak of a single degree of freedom). Because of this unique explanatory variable, we speak of a univariate model, as opposed to multivariate models, which use several variables.

The usefulness of this section is more educational than scientific because, in fact, you will rarely use univariate models. However, their simplicity makes it possible to introduce notions that can become complex when one places oneself in the general framework. Thus, we will notably introduce the construction of the cost function, which measures the error that we make by approximating our data. We will see that finding the best parameters of our model is equivalent to minimizing this cost function. Finally, we will introduce a method of a numerical resolution whose intuition is already in the work of the very venerable Isaac Newton: the descent of gradient.

This section will, therefore, explain the three steps required to pass raw data to the best univariate linear regression model:

- The definition of a hypothesis function;
- Then building a cost function;
- And finally, the minimization of this cost function.

Once these notions have been acquired, we will be able to introduce more efficient linear algorithms.

Defining the Hypothesis Function

In the case of the univariate linear regression, we take a very strong simplifying assumption: the model depends on a single explanatory variable, named X. This variable is an input of our problem, something we know. For example, the number of rooms in an apartment, the atmospheric pressure, the income of your customers, or any size that you think would influence a target, which will be named Y and which, to continue our examples, would be, respectively, the price of an apartment, the number of milliliters of rain fell, or the amount of the average purchase basket of your customers.

We then try to find the best hypothesis function, which we will call h, whose function is to approximate the output values Y:

Contingent on the linear regression with a variable, the hypothesis function h will be of the form:

$h(X) = \theta_0 + \theta_1 X$

In matrix representation, θ_0 and θ_1 form a vector Θ such that:

Our problem is therefore to find the best pair ($\theta 0$, $\theta 1$) such that h(x) is

"close "of Y for the pairs (x, y) of our database, which we can begin to call learning base since the data you have will be used to train the hypothesis function h.

The concept of proximity that has just been introduced encourages quite naturally calculating an error function. Indeed, for each point xi, the hypothesis function associates a value defined by h (xi) which is more or less close to yi. We thus define "the unit error" for xi by (h (xi) - yi) 2 (squaring to make sure that the contribution of the error will penalize a cost function).

Here we have to understand a very important thing: although h is a function of x, J is not! Indeed, the values of x and y are given, and J is by construction a function of the parameters of h, namely ($\theta 0$, $\theta 1$).
Recall for the exercise the meaning of the parameters of J, which define an affine straight line as we were taught in college:

- θ_0 is the ordinate at the origin of the function h, the value of h when x is zero;

- θ_1 is the slope (or coefficient) of h in an orthonormal Cartesian coordinate system, i.e. the variation of h when x increases by one.

At each point in space (θ_0, θ_1), therefore, corresponds to a single line h with its intercept and slope.

Minimizing the cost function

Thus find the best parameters (θ_0, θ_1) h - and therefore the best right to model our problem - exactly equivalent to finding the minimum of the function J.

To understand the function J, note that:

- For θ_0 given, J is a function of $\theta_1$2;

- For θ_1 given, J is a function of θ 2.

For one of these two dimensions, that is to say by fixing one of these two parameters, the function J is a parabola. Taking into account the two dimensions, that is to say by placing oneself in space (θ_0, θ_1), J will thus have a very characteristic bowl shape.

With this form of a bowl, J has a very interesting mathematical property: it is convex. As a reminder, a function f is convex when it satisfies the following property.

In current French, if x_1 and x_2 are two points of the graph of the function f, then the segment [x_1, x_2] is above this same graph.

The set of points above the graph of the function f, in turn, define a convex set, geometric object very simple to understand.

The importance of the convexity of the cost function lies in the method used to minimize it.

Indeed, one way to find the best pair (θ_0, θ_1), is the gradient descent, an iterative method whose principle is quite intuitive: what would a ball drop quite high in our bowl? It would take, at every moment, the best slope to the lowest point of the bowl. The mathematical formulation of this intuition is:

- Iteration 0: initialization of a pair (θ_0, θ_1);
- iterate to convergence:

At each iteration, we choose the best "slope" on our function J to go iteration after iteration to the minimum of our function.

The speed of convergence will depend in particular on the more or less successful initialization of the iteration 0. That is not the real problem. In the case of a non-convex function, an unfortunate initialization can lead to finding a local minimum for J.

At a pair (θ_0, θ_1) found thanks to a local minimum of J corresponds a function h, which is far from optimal. The convexity of J solves this thorny problem because, for a convex function, any local minimum is also the global minimum.

You have probably noticed the presence of a factor α in front of the partial derivative of J in the formulation of the gradient descent. This factor α, which we call the learning rate, physically represents the speed at which we want to finish our iterations. The α larger the greater the step between two iterations, but the greater the probability of overriding the minimum or even diverging. Conversely, the smaller α is, the more likely it is to find the minimum, but the longer the convergence.

As the reader is reassured, he will never have to encode his own gradient descent because all the tools machine learning that use this optimization method make it transparent. On the other hand, it will often be up to him to choose the meta- parameters like α.

Multivariate linear regression

If you have just read the preceding section, you will see that this section is only a generalization of the principles evoked in the univariate case.

We will use this chapter to introduce two new concepts: the standardization of data and an analytical resolution method to find the best parameters of the model.

The model in detail

In the case of univariate linear regression, we look for the best hypothesis function that will approximate the input data:

On the other hand, we offer more variables at the beginning of the problem, which constitutes as many degrees of freedom at the function h to better approximate the input data (remember that the assumption of approximating a quantity with only one variable is an extremely strong hypothesis and is rarely efficient).

Given these new assumptions, h takes a more general form for n input variables:

$$h(X) = \theta_0 + \theta_1 X_1 + \theta_2 X_2 + \ldots \theta_n X_n$$

Our input data is represented easily in the form of a matrix of dimension (m,n), as presented in the chapter "The BA-ba of the data scientist ":

x_{ij} corresponds to the value taken by the variable j of the observation i.

The cost function is again a simple generalization of what we have seen previously.

Moreover, to minimize J, we can use the general method of the gradient descent that we recall:

- iteration 0: initialization of a vector (θ_0, θ_1, θ_2, ..., θ_n)
- iterate until convergence:

J being always convex, we will not have local minima problem. On the other hand, and this is the novelty of this chapter, we run the risk of encountering a problem with this method of resolution if our variables evolve with very different scales.

Chapter 3: Why Use Python for Machine Learning

Python has fast become a very popular programming language around the world as it can be used to write simple and efficient applications.

Python is one of the most beginner-friendly languages, with its simplicity and readability making it easy to understand and grasp. The numerous libraries and packages that are available to simplify the achievement of complex functions with minimal code.

Machine learning applications typically work with large data sets and inbuilt libraries like Numpy, SciPy, and TensorFlow which make Machine Learning and Deep Learning applications much easier to build.

Since Python can be extended to work best for different programs, data scientists have begun to use it to analyze data. It is best to learn how to code in Python since it will help you analyze and interpret data and efficiently identify the best solutions for your business.

Python is a well-designed programming language with a very clean and simple syntax that was developed to work across multiple devices, and it is very intuitive and easy to learn for anyone.

Python is a top-notch programming language that has been designed by none other than Guido van Rossum in the late 1980s, and it is highly popular within the developer community, with beginners and pros alike due to its design philosophy.

Some of the reasons why the python philosophy makes it a truly brilliant language are the following:

Simple and Easy to Learn:

Python is developed to be simple and minimalistic, with any program written by python looking like pseudocode written in English, making it easier for anyone to understand the program. Syntax and keywords that are more English-like also make it easier to learn.

This quality of it is actually the real power of the language, as it allows the programmer to focus on solving the problem rather than trying to learn the syntax and how to use it, a barrier that most of the other high-level languages come with.

High-level Language:

Python is a programming language that is of the highest level. This means that as a developer, many of the internal details such as memory management are abstracted from you and are automatically taken care of by the language, thus making it a language that is very easy to learn for non-programmers/ beginners.

Open Source:

Python is a programming language that is costless open source, which means you that you may write and distribute code written with Python, enabling code written in this language to thrive among the developer community. Therefore, Python code is constantly well maintained, improved, and reused by developers across the world.

Portable:

As mentioned in the introduction, the reason why Python is great as a first programming language to learn is not only due to its simplicity, but also due to it is very powerful, considering that it is designed to work on multiple platforms without requiring any new changes when moving between devices, as long as necessary care is taken to avoid any system-dependent coding.

The range of platforms on which Python code can run includes Windows, Solaris, Macintosh, FreeBSD, VMS, Palm OS, Linux, VxWorks, and even PlayStation!

Interpreted:

Python is an interpreted language like Java - this means that any program written in Python does not need to be compiled every time it needs to be executed. Instead, it can be compiled once and then executed on any number of devices. For example, a program written in C or C++, which are compiler-based, gets converted from the source code (in human-readable format) to binary code (0' s or 1' s machine-readable format) using various platform-specific flags and options. This binary code is then loaded to the device' s memory using what we call the linker/loader, and then it starts running. The compiler/ linker/ loader is, therefore, additional overhead which can be avoided by using languages like Python, as it does not compile source code to binary format; instead, it is designed to be directly executed from the source code.

Internally, the source code gets converted to an intermediate form called the bytecode, which is then interpreted and executed by the device. This feature is what makes Python a useful powerful language, by allowing users to create code once and then use it across a plethora of devices without worrying about compilation and library linking overloads; all you need to do is copy the program files to the device to get started.

Object-Oriented:

Like any modern language, Python embraces an object-oriented programming approach, where the code is organized in classes that act as a template and "objects" which are instances of these classes. Objects are essentially the building blocks of an Object-Oriented Programming language program that combines data and the methods that perform functions upon this data. However, unlike Java or C++, an Object-Oriented Programming System is used in a very easy and powerful way in Python, without over-complicating the concepts.

Fast and Efficient to Use:

Another factor that makes Python a very useful programming language is the fact that it is able to execute any action required extremely quickly. In addition, any piece of code written in Python can be embedded and executed like a script, within programs written in other languages like C or C++. Alternatively, one can write simple python scripts to execute C/ C++ programs.

Batteries Included:

The speed of the execution and writing code, as well as the numerous inbuilt libraries and data types available, enable many complex operations to be achieved in fewer lines of code than with any other programming language, thus simplifying the programmer' s job. This aspect of pre-loaded libraries that come bundled within Python is popularly referred to as "Batteries Included" .

The Python library is so vast that it allows the developer to focus on thinking of a solution to a problem, rather than thinking about how to implement the data Structures and other low-level details involved in finding a solution. The libraries cover almost everything, from working with HyperText Markup Language to databases to audio files (.wav), to Graphical User Interface and to security using cryptography and other utilities.

When it comes to Machine Learning, Python comes with highly efficient in-built libraries that take care of the complexity of implementation, thereby allowing the developer to focus on the actual Machine Learning Model, the actual goal of the system.

Numpy, Panda and SciKit Learn

The main step in Machine learning is data analysis, which Python provides several useful packages.

Several of these libraries can be used in Machine Learning. Some of the most commonly used ones are the following:

Numpy: A commonly used package that is very popular in scientific computing applications. It is primarily used in mathematical and logical operations involving linear algebra, random number generation, Fourier transforms and shape transformations.

A key feature of this package is its support for array data structures, particularly multidimensional arrays and operations on each element.

<u>Pandas</u>: A very popular open-source package that equips Python programming with high-performance data structures and data analysis tool, thus cutting down implementation time significantly. The key data structures supported by this package are series, data frames, and panels.

<u>Matplot Lib</u>: This is a library that is very handy for the purpose of visualizations, useful to develop graphs, charts, etc. Some of the interactive data visualizations this library can create include but are not limited to histograms scatter plots, pie charts, bar graphs, etc.

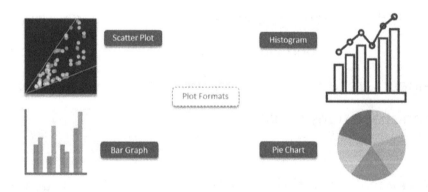

Another sophisticated option for generating such visualizations is a library called "seaborn", which gives a more accurate plot.

The star among all the library packages available in Python is "ScikitLearn", and it is probably one of the key reasons for Python being the most favored machine learning application.

ScikitLearn: This package, built using Numpy and Matplotlib offers a comprehensive way to build simple yet efficient data mining and analysis systems for various applications such as classification, clustering, regression and dimensionality reduction.

To summarize, Python offers an end-to-end solution in order to build machine-learning systems from data wrangling to feature extraction, modeling, training and evaluating the system to visualizations. In addition, it is able to easily integrate with BigQuery, Kafka, pubsub, redshift, etc for data pipeline.

Data wrangling can be achieved using Panda, Numpy and Pyspark, which can be integrated from other big data engines, with Dask being Python's own big data engine.

Python offers a large inbuilt image and video library that comes in handy in the feature extraction phase. This aspect is another one of the many reasons why Python is the preferred language for Machine Learning systems.

The SciKit learning package also helps in various stages, such as building the model and training the model to evaluate the system, making the whole pipeline come together seamlessly. Pytorch is a good alternative for beginners.

TensorFlow is another key package used in Deep Learning applications, and it is more mature than libraries available in R, the main competitor.
Once this is all used to build, train and test the system, Python offers equally effortless options to deploy these systems to production, and creating a REST-API and serializing the model is quite simple with Python.

Therefore, this philosophy, which stresses on a minimalist approach by giving clear syntaxes and keywords in simple English, enables the same task to be done in fewer lines of code in comparison to any other programming languages, mainly C++ or Java. The ease of readability of code and the availability of a loaded library of predefined functions, as well as many data types such as lists and dictionaries, make it a very popular choice to work with.

Trivia: The most popular version of Python' s language functionalities is internally implemented using C.

Chapter 4: Basics of Python Programming

In the chapter we will learn to program with Python from scratch, beginning with system pre-requisites to installing, including everything one would need to know to begin programming in Python. In addition, it includes a section focusing on packages one needs to familiarize with to build machine-learning systems. Let us get started.

The Console IPython

We use IPython as the console where we will interactively execute commands that through Python the computer executes (the I in IPython is interactive). IPython is an interface that allows us to communicate instructions to Python interactively.

When console IPython is activated, it establishes an interface that sends the instructions that we write to the computational infrastructure Python. One way to convince ourselves that this works like this is to realize that IPython is not installed if Python has not been previously installed. That is, while IPython depends on Python, it does not require IPython to be used.

We started console by IPython opening a terminal or command console (which we achieved, if we are using Linux Ubuntu we simultaneously press the keys CTRL, ALT, and T on the keyboard of our computer. Simultaneously press ALT and F2, type gnome-terminal and press ENTER or RETURN) where we execute the command which presents (in the same console where we execute the command) an entry from where we can begin to interact with Python.

Before continuing, it is important to mention that the instruction --pylab is optional, which means that it is not necessary to write it and that we can start console IPython simply by executing the ipython command without being followed by --pylab. Including this option makes it easier to execute operations without having to make them available in console IPython directly, such as displaying on-screen graphics, saving us some scriptwriting.

Some Errors for Not Following the Rules of Python

Before starting to use console IPython (and in order to minimize unnecessary errors) we must understand that Python is very strict in the syntax it understands. As it happens in Linux, the commands must be written in the exact form that corresponds to them, respecting capital letters, lowercase letters or any punctuation they may contain.

So, to avoid unnecessary errors and familiarize ourselves with the issues in Python when receiving instructions with syntax or other errors, take a look at the list of most common responses Python protests when we try to execute commands that contain errors Python does not understand:

Indentation Error: this is one of the errors on the part of Python that appears frequently and is due to blank spaces that are left at the beginning of each instruction that we write in console IPython. While blank spaces are ignored when they appear between instructions, they have the meaning of defining a block of instructions when they are used at the beginning of each line to write the instructions that form a block.

Example

In [1]: 3 + 5

Indentation Error: unexpected indent

If you need to paste code into IPython, try the functions.

In [2]:

This is an error because we started the writing the instruction (consisting of trying to execute the sum 3 + 5) with blank spaces (one or more) at the beginning of the instruction, which indicates the position cursor input symbol following the in [1]. Note that this error is recognized by the issuance of part of Python the message 'Indentation Error: unexpected indent' .

To correct this error we simply remove the blanks at the beginning of the instruction (note that Python ignores the blanks before and after the + sign):

In [2]: 3 + 5

Out [2]: 8

In [3]:

In this case, the instruction that we must correct contains a few characters that are quick to rewrite. When the code that we must correct is longer in the number of characters it contains, we can use the trick of copying and pasting the desired instruction.

At this point, it is important to emphasize that the message Indentation Error should NOT be interpreted as an "error" in the conventional sense of the word. Rather, we should internalize it as a message that Python cannot correctly interpret the instruction it has received and that we should review it to do it correctly. That is to say, Python informs us that something that it does not understand has happened and it issues the alert IndentationError that guides us to correct it. However, remember that the computer is not there to correct the instructions we give it. If that were the case, we would be at their mercy. Computers are to execute literally all the instructions that we give, and we must do so by following the rules (syntax and grammar) that the language we are using to communicate with them imposes, which in the case of this book is the programming Python language. When we find that the computer gives us an incorrect result, we must remember that this happens because we have transmitted the wrong instructions, which do not correspond to the correct instructions for the computer to give us the correct result.

A type of error in the conventional sense of the word and where the computer cannot help us to correct is when we make a wrong account for a sign error, a wrong division, and poor organization of terms in a given expression or a set of steps of wrong computation (the implementation of a wrong algorithm).

The validation of the results obtained with the execution of a program is a recurring theme in this book, which we will deal with frequently in subsequent topics.

NameError: This error also occurs frequently and refers to trying to use a symbol (or variable name) that Python does not know. This is illustrated in the following entry:

In [8]: a

------------------------------------ --------------------------

Name Error   Traceback (most recent call last)
/ home / srojas / Mis_ programas_ python / <ipython - input -2 -60 b725f10c9c> in <module> (
----> 1 to
Name Error: name 'a' is not defined In [9]:

With this error (qualified by the word NameError: name A is not defined), Python is telling us that the symbol or variable is unknown, not assigned any previous definition to use to try to give instructions to execute and assign.

To correct this error we just add value to the variable a as indicated in the line of In [9], in the box that follows: The same sign should be read as assigned to the left side that which is on the right side, is not an equal in the mathematical sense, as illustrated in the entry In [10], where the variable a has now been assigned the value it had previously, plus an additional unit, which can be displayed by simply typing the name of the variable a and pressing RETURN or ENTER (as shown in the output Out [10]). That is, the new value assigned or stored in variable a is number nine. In the input In [12], we multiply the assigned value in the variables a (which is 9) and b (which is 6), as reflected by the result in Out [12].

In [8]: a = 8
In [9]: a = a + 1 In [10]: a
Out [10]: 9
In [11]: b = 6
In [12]: a * b
Out [12]: 54
In [13]:
SyntaxError: this error occurs when we do not finish correctly any instructions that Python must execute. In the case of In [3]: in the next session in the console IPython, the statement with a quote was missing, as indicated in the command In [4]:
In [3]: "Hello

File" <ipython - input -3 - d 2991277 a 5 d 9> ", line 1"

Hello

^

Syntax Error: EOL while scanning string literal

In [4]: "Hello"

Out [4]: 'Hello'

In [5]:

Note the symbol, Which Python writes pointing to the letter "a". This is a help that Python provides, indicating where we can look to find the error.

TypeError: This error occurs when we want to combine objects that are different in nature. Python classifies the entities that it manipulates into objects. We know the type of some entity using the method or function type, which we illustrate in the following lines of code:

In [15]: type (1) Out [15]: int

In [16]: type (1. 5) Out [16]: float

In [17]: type ("Hello") Out [17]: str

In [18]: type (True) Out [18]: bool

In [19]:

Notice that the type of an integer number (such as 1) is int (for an integer type object), that of any real number is float (for a floating-point type object), that of a string of characters (such as "Hello") is str (for a string or string type object), and that of the reserved word of the or Boolean Python Truetype is of type bool (for a logical or Boolean object). A complete list of the types of objects that come with the language is found in the user manual, although the programmer can extend that list by building their own type of objects, as did the developers of NumPy. Therefore, when we try to combine objects of different nature for which Python does not know a rule of how to combine them then TypeError occurs, as we show next:

```
In [5]: type ('a) - = bcd') Out [5]: str
In [6]: type (2) Out [6]: int
In [7]: 2 + 'a) - = bcd'
```

---------------------- ---

```
Type Error                      Traceback (most recent last call)
<ipython - input -7 -6 e98fd07ad31> in <module> ()
----> 1 2 + 'a) - = bcd'
```

Type Error: unsupported operand type (s) for +: 'int' and 'str' In [7]:

The TypeError occurs because we try to add to the whole "2" the characters or string

"á) - = bcd '", which is an operation that Python does not know how to execute.

ZeroDivisionError: this error occurs when in any operation zero divides it:

In [14]: 4/0

----------------------------------- -----------------------------------

Zero Division Error　　　　Traceback (most recent last call)

<ipython - input -14 -6 de94738d89d> in <module> ()

----> 1 4/0

Zero Division Error: integer division or module by zero In [14]:

IndexError: this error occurs when we exceed the limits of objects that in Python are encoded with indexes, such as list, tuple, and dictionary:

In [19]: milista = [10, 2, -3]

In [20]: milista [0]

Out [20]: 10

In [21]: milista [2]

Out [21]: -3

In [22]: milista [4]

---------- --

Index Error   Traceback (most recent last call)

<ipython - input - 22 - 7936870 fb529> in <module> ()

----> 1 milista [4]

Index Error: list index out of range In [23]:

ValueError: this error occurs when you we give a function an incorrect value, or we try to obtain some value outside the limits of a list, tuple and dictionary object. Continuing with the session IPython of the previous section, we have:

In [23]: milista. index (2)

Out [23]: 1

In [24]: milista. index (4)

-- ----------------

Value Error   Traceback (most recent last call)

<ipython - input -26 -379 fe2d3c134> in < module> ()

----> 1 milista. index (4) Value Error: 4 is not in the list

In [25]:

Although it is not noticeable in these interactive calculations, the natural behavior of Python is that when it finds some instruction it does not understand, it generates an error alert and stops the execution of the operation it performs.

In subsequent chapters, we will present bifurcation instructions (such as if-else) through which we can take advantage of the structure of these error messages to guide Python. Instead of stopping the execution of some program, continue with the execution of other instructions that are part of the program when it finds these errors.

Interactive computing in the console IPython
Now let us execute a computation session in the console IPython that we can compare with what we do in any calculator:

Sum:
In [1]: 3 + 5
Out [1]: 8

Subtraction (subtraction):

In [2]: 2 -6

Out [2]: -4

Multiplication (note that the symbol for this purpose is *):

In [3]: 2 * 7

Out [3]: 14

Division:

In [4]: 6 / 2

Out [4]: 3

The operations of addition, subtraction, and multiplication behave in a similar way to how familiar we are with a calculator. With division, however, it must be executed with some care. For example (this happens in Python version 2),

In [5]: 1/3

Out [5]: 0

This result can make us raise our eyebrows and think that the computer has some problem. The following section discusses in some detail why the computer tells us that

1/3=0. To obtain the expected result (the same one that we obtain by making the manual account or with any functional calculator), we must represent the numbers with a decimal point in the form either 1.0 or 1. (It is recommended that we represent the numbers with the decimal point when the integer operation is not necessary)

In [6]: 1.0/3
Out [6]: 0.3333333333333333
We can also group operations using parentheses (in Python brackets and keys are used for other functions)
In [7]: ((2 + 7 * (234 - 15) + 673) * 775) / (5 + 890. 0 - (234 + 1) * 5. 0)
Out [7]: - 6111. 428571428572

We recommend the use of parentheses to instruct Python to perform the arithmetic operations that we want to run first. That is, when Python executes arithmetic operations, it first performs the ones that are in parentheses and then executes the operations of division, multiplication and addition or subtraction. Thus, using parentheses, we can guide Python to execute arithmetic operations in the proper order or in the order that we want.

We can use blank spaces to make what we write more readable:

In [8]: ((2.0 + 7 * (234 - 15) + 673) * 775) / (5 + 890.0 - (234 + 1) * 5.0) Out [8]: - 6111.428571428572

If the expressions we are writing are very long, we can use the diagonal ("symbol slash inverted" "\" (without the quotes) to tell Python that the instruction continues on the next line (we should only avoid including blank spaces at the beginning of the continuation of the instruction). The console IPython indicates that a line is the continuation of the previous one using four points followed by a colon "", as shown below

In [9]: ((2.0 + 7 * (234 - 15) + 673) * 775) \
...: / (5 + 890. 0 - (234 + 1) * 5. 0) Out [9]: - 6111. 428571428572 Power

Operations (or enhancement) are represented by the symbol. Thus, x raised to the power y (xy) in Python is written xy (we must be careful to review what we write, lest instead of power we write a multiplication).

In [10]: 2. 5 ** 3
Out [10]: 15. 625
In [11]: 2. 5 ** (3. 2 + 2.1)
Out [11]: 128. 55294964201545

In some cases, as in the previous one, the output presented by Python resembles the way a calculator does. In other cases, Python represents it in the form (decimal number) (letter e) (sign ±) (number), as in the case:

In [12]: 6.78 ** 30
Out [12]: 8.647504884825773 e ± 24
In this example, we must observe that (used in this way), the letter e represents the power base 10, as we can verify in the following session of IPython:
In [13]: 8.647504884825773 e +24 - 8.647504884825773 * 10 ** 24 Out [13]: 0.0

In [14]: 1 e + 2

Out [14]: 100. 0

In [15]: 1 e2

Out [15]: 100. 0

In [16]: 1e -2

Out [16]: 0.01

In [17]:

This allows us to write $20000.0 = 2.0 \times 10^4$ as:

In [14]: 2 e4

Out [14]: 20000.0

We can also use non-integer exponents. For example, to obtain the square or cube root of an expression we can do it in the form:

In [15]: 4 ** (1. / 2.)

Out [15]: 2.0

In [16]: 4 ** 0.5

Out [16]: 2.0

In [17]: 8 ** (1. / 3.)

Out [17]: 2.0

In [18]: 8 ** 0.3333

Out [18]: 1.999861375368307

We see in Out [18]: that 80.3333 approximates the √3 8. The reader can experience finding how the three are needed to approximate one third to find the expected value of √3 8.

Make calculations involving trigonometric, hyperbolic, logarithmic and exponentials is a bit more elaborate. By default, Python does not include resources in memory to perform calculations with these functions (as it does for the operations we have presented so far and many others). Therefore, to make calculations with these transcendental functions, we must tell Python to put in the computer's memory resources to do those calculations. In this book, we will use the module NumPy for this purpose.

How do we use these functions?
The first thing we should know is that Python interprets the argument of these functions as angles expressed in radians. That is, √si want to calculate the sine of the angle of sixty degrees (60o)we know is within(60o)=3/2, in Python must first express that angle in radians and then

get the value within resultant. Transcendent functions in Python via NumPy.

To convert a given angle in degrees to radians, we multiply the angle in degrees by the value of the constant π = 3.1415926 and we divide the result by 180. To avoid making this conversion account, the module NumPy already contains a function named radiansconverts that are given value in degrees to radians. Now let's illustrate how we can use these functions doing the calculation of the sine of sixty degrees (remember that the number m in the bracket of the symbols In [m]: of the console IPython does not have to be consecutive to the one we have been using. that the reader, one may have gone to take a break by closing the session of IPython and then start a new one. With this, we mean that the numbering of In [m]: is irrelevant at the time of executing the instructions).

First, we must invoke or bring to the working memory of IPython the functionality of the module NumPy. We do this using the import command, in the form (remember to press the key ENTER or RETURN at the end of writing np):

In [68]: import numpy as np

In [69]:

We should note that in this case, after executing the import statement, is not generated in the console IPython an output line Out [68]:. This is because we do not expect any output value as a result of executing the import command (only an error message will be issued (with the name ImportError) in case the module to be brought into memory does not exist. executing the previous instruction using the wrong name of the module NumPy:

In [69]: import Numpy as np

--- --------------------

Import Error   Traceback (most recent last call)

<ipython - input -1 - 8 bef5f2b877b> in <module> ()

----> 1 import Numpy as np

Import Error: No module named Numpy In [70]:

Once the functionality of the module NumPy is available in the working memory of IPython, we can use the functions, preceding their names with the sequence "np."(Not including the quotes.) The point is also part of the sequence.

To demonstrate how we use these functions, we will first convince ourselves that to calculate the sine of an angle the function without requires that the angle is expressed in radians. To do this, we will directly calculate the sine of the given value, without doing any conversion. That is, we will pass to the function without the value of sixty to see what results:

In [85]: np. sin (60 .0)
Out [85]: - 0. 30481062110221668
The output Out [85]: -0.30481062110221668 is a negative value, and this indicates us that this can be the value of the sine of the sixty-degree angle, (which we already know is 3/2. Now calculate the sine of the angle but converting it first to radians:

In [86]:   np. pi
Out [86]:   3. 141592653589793.0

In [87]:   (60* np. Pi) / 180

Out [87]:   1. 0471975511965976

In [88]:   np. sin (Out [87])

Out [88]:   0. 8660254037844386

In [89]:   np. sqrt (3) / 2

Out [89]:   0. 8660254037844386

In [90]:   np. sin ((60. 0 * np.pi) / 180

Out [90]:   0. 8660254037844386

In [91]:   np. radians (60)

Out [91]:   1 .0471975511965976

In [92]:   np. sin (np. radians (60))

Out [92]:   0 .8660254037844386

In this account, we first show with the output cell Out [86]: that np.pi contains an approximation of the numerical value corresponding to the number π. Then, in In [87]: we convert the angle of sixty degrees to its value in radians (as we already mentioned, to make that conversion we multiply the angle in degrees by the value of the number π and the result we divide it by 180) and the value that results and is stored or assigns to the output cell Out [87]: we calculate the sine in In [88]:.

The result in Out [88]: must correspond to the bosom of sixty degrees. This verified what we are calculating in In [89]: the decimal value of 3/2, as we know, is within the angle of sixty degrees. Effectively, both Out [88]: and Out [89]: results are the same.

In the input cells In [90]: and In [92]: we show that the entire process can be executed in a single instruction. The line In [91]: tells us that the function radians effectively converts given angles in degrees to radians and, therefore, the function radians should only be used to make that conversion.

In Python, we can also operate with complex numbers without further complication. A complex number has a real part and an imaginary part. Recall that the so-called imaginary unit is a value such that its square is equal to 1, which in Python is represented by the combination "1j" (without quotes). Let us look at some operations with the complex number 2 + 3j (note that the real part is 2, while the imaginary part is 3j):

```
In [1]: 2 + 3 j

Out [1]: (2 + 3 j)

In [2]: (2 + 3 j) + (2 -3 j)

Out [2]: (4 + 0 j)

In [3]: (2 + 3 j) - (2 -3 j)

Out [3]: 6 j

In [4]: (2 + 3 j) * (2 -3 j)

Out [4]: (13+ 0 j)

In [5]: (2 + 3 j) / (2 -3 j)

Out  [5]:  (-  0.    38461538461538464    +    0.
9230769230769231 j)

In [6]: np. sqrt (-2)

/ home / srojas / and Prog / Anaconda / bin / ipython: 1:
Runtime Warning: invalid

value encountered in sqrt

\ #! / home / srojas / my Prog / Anaconda / bin / python

Out [6]: nan

In [7]: np. sqrt (-2 + 0 j)

Out [7]: 1. 4142135623730951 j

In [8]: np. lib. scimath sqrt (-2)

Out [8]: 1. 4142135623730951 j

In [9]: from numpy. lib. scimath import sqrt as csqrt
```

In [10]: csqrt (-2)

Out [10]: 1. 4142135623730951 j

In the input cell In [1]: simply, we type the number to see what answers Python, who in Out [1]: recognizes the combination by putting it in parentheses (this operation should not be confused with an object that in python is known as a "tuple" and that we will study later). Then, in In [2]: until In [5]: we do the fundamental procedure of addition, subtraction, multiplication, and division between two complicated numbers, whose results Out [2]: - Out [5]: can be verified by computation manual. In [6]: the error obtained when trying to calculate the square root of a negative number is presented, while in In [7]: we indicate a way to obtain the respective result. Another way to achieve this result is by using the library, scimath Numpy that is illustrated in In [8]: In [9]: we present a way to extract from the library scimath the function we need, giving it a more convenient name (csqrt), to avoid overwriting any other function sqrt that may be available with that name in memory current IPython. The reader should compare the different ways of obtaining the square root of a negative number presented in the input cells In [7]: In [9]: and In [10]: This possibility of executing some operation using different resources helps us to verify results when we present any doubt about it, or we want to ratify it by some other means. This is an advantage offered by the wide variety of computer libraries available in Python.

Python also offers the possibility to perform operations with fractions of whole numbers in an exact way, without resorting to the module SymPy that also offers such functionality. To do this we must make available in the session IPython the function or method of the fractions module called Fraction, which allows executing such operations. To use this function, the fractions, numerator and denominator is written in the Fraction form (numerator, denominator), as illustrated below:

In [18]:   from fractions import Fraction

In [19]:

Out [19]:   Fraction (5, 4) + Fraction (5, 4)

Fraction (5, 2)

In [20]:

Out [20]:   Fraction (5 * 13 * 11 * 24, 4 * 13 * 76 * 25)

Fraction (33, 190)

In [21]:

Out [21]:   Fraction (5 * 13 * 11 * 24, 4 * 13 * 76 * 25)

Fraction (541, 380)   +   Fraction (5, 4)

In [23]:

Out [23]:   19 * Fraction (33, 190) + 3 +

25/10 Fraction (83, 10)

In [24]:

Out [24]:   19 * Fraction (33, 190) + 3 + 2.5

8.8

In [25]:

We assign it as an activity for the reader to execute the indicated operations manually and verify that the results in the output cells Out [19]: to Out [24]: are correct.

Calculating In Python with Extended Numerical Precision

Having the ability to execute operations with fractions accurately is just one of the potentials that Python offers and that can only be found in some high-cost calculators.

An example that illustrates other computing potentials that Python puts at the disposal of the programmer is found in the example of the chessboard that appears in the book 'The Man Who Calculated' . We know that a chessboard contains 64 squares. An account of the referred book tells that the inventor of the game was offered to choose a prize for his invention. The inventor of the game requested that each square of the chessboard be given rice grains equivalent to number two raised to the power of the number corresponding to the square of the board minus one (considering the squares of the chessboard have been numbered one at sixty-four).

Thus, starting with square one, the inventor should receive 21-1 = 20 = 1 grain of rice. Then, through box two, the inventor should receive 22-1 = 21 = 2 grains of rice; through box three, I would receive 22 = 4 grains of rice; through box four, I would get 23 = 8 grains of rice and so on, until you reach square 64, by which the inventor would receive 263 = 9223372036854775808 grains of rice. We leave it as an exercise for the reader to verify in his calculator (or by any other means to calculate differently Python) the number of grains of rice corresponding to square 64 of the chessboard. Then, we invite you to verify the result of the total number of grains of rice that the inventor of the chessboard should have received and that is not more than the sum of the amount of grains of rice received for each square of the board. In Python, that sum can be written in the form:

```
In [14]: 2 ** 0 + 2 ** 1 + 2 ** 2 + 2 ** 3 + 2 ** 4 + 2 ** 5 + 2
** 6 + 2 ** 7 + 2 ** 8 + 2 ** 9 + 2 ** 10 + \...: 2 ** 11 + 2 **
12 + 2 ** 13 + 2 ** 14 + 2 ** 15 + 2 ** 16 + 2 ** 17 + 2 **
18 + 2 ** 19 + 2 ** 20 + \...: 2 ** 21 + 2 ** 22 + 2 ** 23 + 2
** 24 + 2 ** 25 + 2 ** 26 + 2 ** 27 + 2 ** 28 + 2 ** 29 + 2
** 30 + \...: 2 ** 31 + 2 ** 32 + 2 ** 33 + 2 ** 34 + 2 * * 35 +
2 ** 36 + 2 ** 37 + 2 ** 38 + 2 ** 39 + 2 ** 40 + \...: 2 ** 41
+ 2 ** 42 + 2 ** 43 + 2 ** 44 + 2 ** 45 + 2 ** 46 + 2 ** 47 +
2 ** 48 + 2 ** 49 + 2 ** 50 + \...: 2 ** 51 + 2 ** 52 + 2 ** 53
+ 2 ** 54 + 2 ** 55 + 2 ** 56 + 2 ** 57 + 2 ** 58 + 2 ** 59 +
2 ** 60 + \...: 2 ** 61 + 2 ** 62 + 2 ** 63
Out [14]: 18446744073709551615 L
In [15]: 2 ** 64 -1
Out [15]: 18446744073709551615 L
```

To be sure that the sum was correctly done in Python, we verified the result by calculating (264 one), whose result is shown in the Outline [14]: In this chapter we show that the sum of $2^0 + 2^1 + 2^2 + + 2^n = 2^{n+1}$ 1, for all integer n 0. By this, we mean that the result obtained is correct and that the reader can corroborate from other sources.

Although we have not yet entered the subject of programming in Python, it is pertinent to present a succinct way of doing the previous account with a little less writing or programming instructions in Python that the computer has to execute. Let us write the following:

In [8]: sum ([2 ** j for j in range (64)]) Out [8]: 18446744073709551615 L

Thus, we can say (without pretending to be rigorous) that programming is the art of writing efficient instructions that the computer understands and can execute by working for us (for example, with this last instruction we save ourselves from transcribing the terms of the sum $2^0 + 2^1 + + 2^{63}$ in the console IPython. If there is an error in the final result, then the culprit is oneself, unless the computer has some failure (such as, for example, malfunction of the RAM memory or CPU warming that makes any computer issues erroneous results).

Note that in this operation we have written the numbers involved without the decimal point. We leave as an exercise that the reader executes the sum including the decimal point in any of the addends (that is, instead of writing 22 type2.02 or 2.2).

The letter L at the end of the integers in the outputs Out [14]: and Out [15]: indicates that Python has used a special method to make those accounts with integers that are called extended precision.

Precision and Representation of Numbers in the Computer

The exercise of using Python to calculate interactively must have given us the idea that in the computer the numbers are represented with a finite number of digits. Something we do for convenience when we say that the number $\pi = 3.1416$, what we do is take a finite number of figures (in this case 5) to represent a number that has an infinite number of figures.

Something similar happens with any computer only with more restriction. With the computer, we can only obtain a finite and fixed number of digits that represent the numbers as best as possible.

This finiteness in the representation of numbers makes some arithmetic operations inaccurate. For example, one expects that $(3)2 = 3$. However, in Python, we find that

```
In [3]: import numpy as np
In [4]: (np. Sqrt (3)) ** 2
Out [4]: 2.9999999999999996
```

That is, the computer gives us an approximation of the exact result. The result of $(\sqrt{3})2 = 2.9999999999999996$ will be the same on any computer that operates with numbers in the binary system with 64 bits of precision, which is the operating environment of Python by default (except for operations with integers that is unlimited, only restricted by the available computer memory or RAM.) To get an idea of what this means, we can calculate in the console IPython (5 1000) (125 2000)) and verify the result manually). Another example would be adding 0.1 say ten times (to0.1 +0.1 +0.1 +0.1 +0.1 +0.1 +0.1 +0.1 +0.1 =0.9999999999999999) that we expect is equal to $10 \times 0.1 = 1$.

The generality of computers stores information in the binary system of zero and one and every zero or one is called a bit. The system we are used to using is the decimal system, in which the representation base is number ten (10) because there are ten digits to represent the numbers from zero (0) to nine (9). In addition, in our manual calculations we can think of any number of combinations of those digits to represent any number (we even use notation as a sign (decimal part) 10 exponent. In a conventional computer (based on binary or base 2 floating-point arithmetic) this is not possible. For example, in computers that operate with number representation in the binary system with 64 bits, it means that there are 64 spaces to store combinations of zeros and ones to represent each number. To store the number sign, 52 spaces are used to store the mantissa, or decimal part of the number and the remaining 11 spaces are used to store the exponent of the number, that is, the numbers are represented in the form sign× mantissa × 2exponent.

Thus, 16 or 17 digits showing the computer when writing (Python) an irrational number such as π or a fraction not ends as 1/3, is because 2-52 2.22 10-16 it is the smallest mantissa we can have with 52 digits in the binary system (base 2), represented in the form 0.00000000000000000000000000000000000000000000 00000012 (the subscript "2" indicates that the number must be represented in the base system "2". In this case, it means 0 2-1 + 0 2-2 + 0 2-3 + + 1 2-52 = 2-52). This means that in the 64-bit representation of the numbers in a computer we can only have confidence in the first 15 digits after the decimal point.

A thorough discussion of how the representation of numbers on the computer is outside the topic coverage of this book. To cover this lack, the references in the chapter list somewhere the reader can consult in depth the subject that is known in the literature as representation and arithmetic of numbers in floating-point.

However, we must be aware that the arithmetic that operates on the computer may not coincide with what we expect, especially when we operate with very small numbers compared to other numbers. We know that $x + 1 > x$. In certain cases, as a consequence of the finite representation of the numbers in the computer, this does not happen, as illustrated in the following example:

In [46]: 2. ** 53
Out [46]: 9007199254740992. 0
In [47]: 9007199254740992. 0 + 1
Out [47]: 9007199254740992. 0

Before presenting other important examples that illustrate how the finite representation of numbers in the computer can infringe other arithmetic operations, we must first introduce a measure that allows us to quantify the error we make when we make approximate calculations in the computer.

Such a measure is the relative error. With it, we can, for example, clearly establish the error that is made when a number is approached either by truncating its infinite representation or by approximating that representation to keep a certain number of digits representing the number in question. If N is accurate is the exact number, and N approx. is your approximation (in a representation) N exact with fewer digits), the relative error (ER) is defined as:

$$ER = .N \text{ Exact} - N \text{ approx.} \ldots (2.1) . \text{ Exact } N.$$

The bars indicate absolute value. Another alternative to approximate 5 to a certain number of digits is to approximate it according to whether the digit to the right of the figure where we are going to make the approximation is greater or less than five. If this is greater than five are, one unit increases the digit where we will make the approximation. If it is less than five, it is left the same.

Following this rule, the number N exact =5/3 can be approximated to take the value of N approx. =1.667. We take this opportunity to comment that these operations can be performed exactly in Python using the module SymPy:

In [1]: from sympy import *
In [2]: (S (5) / 3 - S (1666) / 1000) / (S (5) / 3) Out [2]: 1/2500
In [3]: (S (5) / 3 - S (1667) / 1000) / (S (5) / 3) Out [3]: - 1/5000

Note the use of the function by S () acting on some integers. In this way, SymPy tells Python to treat the number, as an integer without approximation, which when divided by another whole number becomes an exact rational number. The operations are executed as fractions of integers.

Now, returning to the approximation errors that computers make when performing operations representing numbers with a finite number of digits, consider the following example in which it is illustrated that the associative property of the sum A + B + C = (A + B) + C = A + (B + C) in the computer can be violated in certain circumstances, when (for example) we operate with the difference between very close numbers and/or we divide between small numbers:

In [49]: A = 0 0254

In [50]: B = 9788. 0

In [51]: ((A + B) ** 2 -2 * A * B- B ** 2) / A ** 2

Out [51]: 1. 0000241431738204

In [52]: ER = abs (1 - 1. 0000241431738204)

In [53]: ER

Out [53]: 2. 4143173820379005 e -05

In [54]: ≈ ×

The result obtained Out [51]: has a relative error of ER = 2.41 10-5 regarding the value that should have been obtained that is one (as can be verified by developing the square that appears in the expression and canceling common terms). The imprecision of this result is due to the fact that in the numerator we subtract two numbers very close to each other that (as the reader can verify) for the given values of A = 0.0254 and B = 9788.0 correspond to the terms $(A + B)^2$ and $2AB + B^2$. Then, making the operation more inaccurate, we divide by a small number (which is A^2). To correct this inaccuracy, we can invert the values assigned to A and B:

In [53]: A = 9788. 0
In [54]: B = 0. 0254
In [55]: ((A + B) ** 2 -2 * A * B- B ** 2) / A ** 2
Out [55]: 1. 0000000000000002
In [56]: ER = abs (1 - 1. 0000000000000002)
In [57]: ER
Out [57]: 2. 220446049250313 e -16

In this case, we see that the relative error is of the order of the precision obtained by the computer in 64-bit operations ER ≈ 2.22 × 10-16. The reader can specify that with the new assignment of values to "A" and "B" are no longer subtracted very similar amounts nor is it divided by a small number.

The intention of these exercises is to alert the reader that before starting any computational project, one must have an idea of the magnitude of the numbers involved in any calculation, this with the intention of avoiding organizing them in a way that magnifies errors that are a consequence of the finite representation of the numbers made by any computer. However, it is convenient to point out that when the system being studied is chaotic, it can generate results that can erroneously be attributed to the floating-point arithmetic on which the operations executed by the computer are based. In spite of how fascinating the subject is, it falls outside the scope of this book.

Installing Python and Getting Started

The first step to learn a language is getting the development environment ready and to dive into writing code snippets. Therefore, to learn Python, we first need to install Python to execute Python programs and text editors, which we can use to write and edit code.

As it is an open-sourced programming language, Python comes pre-installed on most of the Linux platforms including Mac, while some Windows systems have Python installed by default.

To verify if Python is installed on your system and ready to be used, type the keyword "Python" on the terminal as follows.

1. Launch the terminal window and in the prompt that appears on the shell, type the following keyword:

>python

2. If Python was installed on your system, the command would print the version details of Python that is available on the system and would launch the interpreter.

On Windows, it' s as simple as running the.exe file, and on Linux, you can either use the package manager to launch installation using binaries or directly download the source file, compile and build your own binaries (depending on RedHat or Ubuntu flavors) following specific, easy to follow and straightforward instructions from the website. Either way, it is advised to download the source code in order to have a copy of it and to further learn more about the in-built libraries.

After completing the installation, you can verify that Python is indeed installed by typing the "python" command on the terminal; the interpreter will print the version of the installed python version and start running. Python' s interactive interpreter is a great tool in itself, useful for learning how to program with Python.

First Program

Once installed, you can quickly verify that everything is set by launching the terminal and typing "python" to launch the interpreter. Remember, Python is an interpreted language where each statement can be interpreted and executed without having to be compiled for each platform separately. An interpreter is an interactive tool that comes pre-bundled with all python installations, which can be used to quickly execute and verify python statements.

The interpreter can be used to execute Python statements and see output immediately, without having to go through the hassle of creating a file and executing it to learn basic python statements. It is also a handy tool when one needs to experiment to correct errors in programming and debug.

Let us now write our infamous "Hello World "program and officially get started with writing programs in Python.

>python
>>>>>>print "Hello World"
Hello World

One statement is all it takes - no fancy imports or function blocks required. The keyword "print," is sufficient to instruct the interpreter to print anything that is enclosed within " " .

Since it is an interpreter-driven language, the same interactive interpreter can double up and be used as a calculator; for example, you can perform basic math operations as follows:

>*python*

>>>>>>*3+5*

>>>>>>*8*

>>>>>>*5-2*

>>>>>>*3*

And so forth. Just play around by executing various python statements directly from the interpreter and check the output to learn the basics. You can exit from the interpreter at any time by using one of the following commands,

>>> *ctrl + d*

Or

>>>*exit()*

Or

```
>>>quit()
```

With Python installed, and after having tested our first piece of code with the programming language, we are all set to delve deeper and explore the magical world of python programming! Let us get rolling!

Basic Program Structure

Now, let us learn some more about the basics of writing longer python code. So far, what we have seen are simple python statements, with many of these cohesive statements forming a code block and many such blocks making up the whole program. Therefore, for more serious programming, it becomes imperative to use a text editor and have the statements bundled together into files. Let us now look at how to create a simple python program and execute it from a file.

The official IDE for python is IDEAL; however, you can use any editor of your choice, like vim, sublime text, notepad, etc. Open a new file and type in the succeeding statement:

print "Hello World"

Now, save the file with the name of your choice, with as.py as the extension, like HelloWorld.py in our case, and you have officially created your first program file with Python.

Now, launch the terminal, navigate to the file path and execute the python script using the following command to execute the file, and watch the program run.

>python./HelloWorld.py

This command basically launches the interpreter and instructs it to take the file named "HelloWorld.py" from the current directory (./) and execute the statements.

>Hello World

The output is now delivered onto the console, so in our case, the string "Hello World" is printed. The file can also be executed by simply typing./HelloWorld.py on the terminal after launching the interpreter.

The python program file can also be executed as follows:

>>> execfile("helloworld.py")

Hello World

The execfile() API will look for the file in the mentioned path, which in our case is the current directory and then run the script.

White Spaces and Indentation

The python statements do not have an end of line delimiters such as the "¡" used in languages like C or C++. When typing the statement "print "Hello World" , it does not require a "¡" to mark its end. This also means that the blocks/statements of a python program are marked by means of spaces and indentation.

Therefore, in any given Python program, white spaces and indentation are extremely important components, and if used incorrectly, could cause errors.

Unlike other languages, white spaces are extremely important in python programming, and if used incorrectly, they could cause some serious errors preventing the execution of the program itself.

White spaces in the beginning mark different blocks of the program. Blocks are differentiated from one another based on indentation, with space before a statement denoting the beginning of a new block, and indent to end the block. In addition, each letter or word is separated using white spaces.

>>>>a = 5
>>>> a = 5
^ a= 5

Unexpected indentation error

The first statement compiles fine (we will learn more about what this statement does in the next chapter), but the second statement will give you an error due to the inappropriately placed extra space at the beginning of the second statement, before the "a". With spaces being so important, as a rule of thumb, the following basic rules should be followed with respect to white lines and indentation to have a uniformly understood code,

- Use 4 spaces to denote indentation

- Do not mix spaces and tab

- Always leave one-line spacing between two functions

- To separate two classes, use two-line spacing

- Comment statements begin with # and are a single line,

#This comment is a single line.

To have multi-line comments in a python file, enclose the statements using triple quotes as follows,

" '

This comment is a multi-line statement for python

" '

Let us now look at a couple more examples using the rules regarding white space and comments that we have learned. Save the following bunch of lines in a .py file and execute them at once, or you can execute them one by one using the interpreter.

print "This is a sample program"

print 3+4 #this prints the sum of the two numbers

#print 3+4 #this statement is itself a comment hence nothing happens.

With the basic rules set, let us now delve deeper and uncover the powerful data types that python offers and how we can use them to write elegant and powerful code.

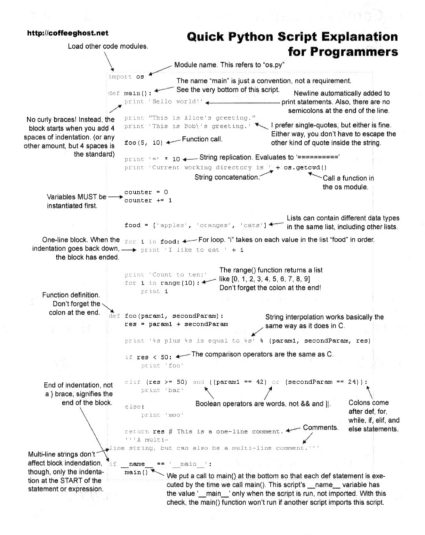

Variable Declaration and Data Types

Having now seen some basic Python statements and coding practice, it is time to learn the next fundamental yet extremely necessary concept – the use of variables.

Variables

Variables are the fundamental building block of a program; they enable to store values and allow a variety of operations to be performed on these values to generate the necessary outcome. For example, say you were doing an addition of two numbers, concatenating two strings, etc. Variables are nothing but placeholders to store values, like in the below statement,

>>>>>>a = 5

Here, A is a variable name that has a memory space assigned to it, and this space will hold the value to the right side of the assignment operator (=), that is 5, which is a number in this case. Unlike other languages, it is not necessary to explicitly declare variables; instead, just by assigning values like in the above, the variable is declared and associated with required memory space.

Python lets users nominate the same value to multiple variables as below,

```
>>>>a=b=c=5
```

Here, all three variables a, b, c get assigned the same value, which is 5. You can also assign different values to different variables in a sequence like below,

```
>>>>a, b, c = 1, 2,  "hello"
```

The above statement assigns the integers 1 to a, 2 to b, and the string "hello" to variable c. That is how simple it is to assign values and use variables with python.

Let us look at an example of using variable names and writing simple python code,

```
>>>>>>a = 5
>>>>>>b = 3
>>>>>>c = a+b
>>>>>>print c
Output: 8
```

The above program declares and assigns an integer value to two variables and uses the + operator to perform addition on these two values, storing the result in another variable 'c' , finally using the "print" keyword to display the result to the console.

Data Types

The type of value stored determines the amount of space required for a variable – number – integer, decimal, character, etc. However, unlike in other high-level programming languages, data types in python do not explicitly precede variables.

Any object has three elements to it –type, identity, and value. The following keyword can be used on any given data type to find its type, which determines what operations are possible to be done on the given object. For example:

>>> type(5)
<type 'int'>

The other useful keyword is an id(), which is used to identify the identity of the given object. This API returns the address of the given object.

Objects created do not need to be explicitly destroyed, but any object that is not reachable is cleared from memory by the garbage collector. Unlike C or C++ where the value is stored in a variable, variables in Python are declared and referred by tags. So, if a = 2 is declared, it is the value "2" which is referred by "a" . Similarly, adding b = 2 in the program will have the same value 2 which is now also tagged by "b" . This is called "tagging" , a property of python variables that enables efficient usage of memory.

There is a beautiful tool available for programmers to visualize how python objects are represented in memory, which helps the developer see what really happens behind the scenes for any given python statement:

http://www.pythontutor.com/visualize.html#mode=edit

Working with Numbers

This data type is used to define and use any numeric value, either integers or floating-point numbers. Any common mathematical operations such as +, -, *, / can be used on numerical objects.

For Example,

Integer

>>>5 + 6

11

>>> 88+12

100

*>>> 25*4*

100

*>>> 100**2*

10000

Floating Point Number

>>>1.5 + 1.5

3

>>> 2.6+2.4

5.0

*>>> 1.5*4*

6.0

>>> 5.5/5.5

1.0

Python supports four different numeric data types – int, float, long and complex.

Int – holder regular integers - 1

Float- to hold floating-point numbers – 1.5

Long – to store long integers – 123458945L

Complex – to store complex numbers of the format x+yj. For example, 2+3j – where 2 is the real number and 3 is the imaginary number.

Note that the data type does not need to explicitly be mentioned when declaring variables. Python implicitly understands the amount of memory required for a variable based on the value assigned. Several common arithmetic operations can be done on the numeric value, and they can quickly be tested on the terminal by launching the interpreter, making the python interpreter act as a calculator.

For example, in the Python Interpreter, you can easily test these operations:

Addition +

Subtraction –

Multiplication *

Division /

Apart from using operators, the programmer can import various packages/libraries, which contain predefined functions that can be applied on data type in order to obtain a required output. For example,

>>>*import math*

>>>*math.sqrt(36)*

6

The above statement imports math library using several operations like sum(), sqrt(), ceil(), floor(), factorial(), pow(), log() etc.

>>> *math.ceil(1.67)*

2.0

>>> *math.floor(1.67)*

1.0

>>> *math.pow(6,2)*

36

The library includes several functions for trigonometric calculations such as sin(), cos(), tan(), radian(), and angle(). To really understand how useful and fundamental these are, let us look at a real-life example:

Example: A program to calculate simple interest

P=100

N=2

R=3

SI=(p*n*r)/100

print SI

Output:6

Reading User Input

One cannot always predetermine and feed input data in programs; instead, many times, the program should have a provision to read user input and take action based on the data received. Let us look at how user input can be read in python.

The two API has provided to achieve this are,

input()

raw_input()

raw_input() takes a string as input data which can be used as a prompt to give instructions to the user on the console and read the input data given.

For Example:

>>>>print (raw_input('What' s your favorite sport? '))

>>>>What' s your favorite sport? #this is the prompt that is printed on the console

>>>>Baseball #this is the user input

>>>> Baseball #this is the output displayed by the print statement.

In addition, the input data can be redirected and saved to a variable and used later for other operations.

For example

>>>>age = raw_input('What is your age? ')

>>>>What is your age? #this is the prompt that gets printed on the console

>>>>25 #this is the user input

>>>>age= age+5 #perform some operation on the input value.

>>>>print ("In 5 years, you will be" +age) #the plus operator is used to concatenate the statement and the value.

>>>>In 5 years, you will be 30

Similarly, the other API input() can also be used to read user input similar to raw_input.

For example

>>>>>age = input('What is your age? ')

>>>>>What is your age?

>>>>>25

>>>>> input('What' s your favorite sport? ')

>>>>>What' s your favorite sport?

>>>>>Baseball

Having learned how to use variables, read inputs and perform basic arithmetic operations, the next important thing to learn is to know how to use python statements to format the output displayed on the console.

The common keyword used to display output is "print" , which takes the expression and redirects it to the standard output. Depending on how the parameters are fed to this, the output is formatted accordingly. Some examples are:

Syntax	Output
print "Hello"	Hello
print "Hello" , "World"	Hello World
print (5, 6)	5 6
a=5 print "value of a: " +a	Value of a: 5

Apart from merely concatenating values, the values itself can be formatted using what we call "format strings", which define the type of data that is getting printed, like string, numeric or decimal numbers. We will look at string formatting more thoroughly in the next chapter.

Working with Strings

The next data type that is most commonly used in any program is the "strings". A string can be declared by enclosing an array of characters within either single or double quotes, while multi-line strings can be declared using triple double-quotes. Python allows several operations such as concatenation and string formatting to be done with the use of simple operators.

Concatenation

As we now know, Python is an object-oriented language, with everything represented as classes and objects of that class. Comes with several inbuilt data type objects and functions that can operate on these objects.

These objects are essentially the building blocks of your program; Python's library is so vast that the programmer can simply focus on the algorithm rather than on how to implement each function.

For example, to concatenate two strings, all it takes is to use the '+' operator,

>*str1 = "Hello"*

>*str1 += "World"*

>*print str1*

Output: Hello World

Or

>*str1 = "Hello"*

>*str2 = "World"*

>*print str1+str2*

Output: Hello World

Thus, the "+" operator is pre-loaded to perform concatenation if the data type is a string. Apart from these pre-defined data types, the users can also define their own, however, most of the times the pre-defined library is sufficient.

Formatting:

The string object can be styled to upper case or lower case easily using the following functions implemented as part of a "string" class/package.

>>> *import string*

>>> *str = "python"*

>>> *string.upper(str)*

'PYTHON

More formatting like left justify, right justify and center can be defined as below,

>>> *str = "left justified"*

>>> *str.ljust(12)*

'left justified'

>>> *str.ljust(25)*

'left justified'

>>> *str.center(25)*

' left justified '

Repetition: To repeat string in python, simply use the * operator, the multiplication used on string type data, which achieves the following:

>>> *str1 = 'Hello'*

>>>str1*2

HelloHello

The * operator repeats the given string the number of times quoted following the operator, in this case twice as the number quoted is 2.

Indexing:

If you are familiar with other programming languages like C or C++, you will remember that strings are nothing but an array of characters, which can be accessed using a subscript of an array, and similarly, python offers multiple string operations by way of indexing as follows:

>>>str1 = 'Hello'

>>>print str1[0]

H

The programmer can thus easily access any range within a given string using the [] operator. This is called indexing; the string array subscript starts with 0 in the forward direction and to access the string in reverse, the subscript is '-1' .

Some More examples:

>>> str = 'pythonWorld'

```
>>> str[1:4]
'yth'
>>> str[-1]
'd'
>>> str[3:]
'honWorld'
```

Slicing:

Now that we saw that indexing could be used to access any character in a string, additionally the colon (:) can be used to slice a range of characters from a given string as follows,

```
>>>str2 =   'World'
>>>print str2[1:3]
Wor
>>>print str2[:-1]
Worl
>>>print str2[-1:]
d
```

A combination of concatenation and slicing can be used to update any given string as follows,

```
>>> print str2[4:]+' Wide'
```

WorldWide

Another useful function while working with strings is the split() function, which can be used to split a string based on a delimiter - by default, "white space" is used as a delimiter.

>>>str = "Hello World "

>>>print str.split()

['Hello' , 'World']

Replace Characters:

One can replace characters within a given string as follows,

>>>str = 'Hello'

>>>str[1:]+" pp" +str[:4]

Heppo

The keywords 'in' and 'not in' can be used to identify if a given character is present in the given string or not, which returns a Boolean answer of 'true' or 'false' .

Also, the str() or repr() functions can be applied to switch values of other data types to strings.

Therefore, strings are a powerful data type object in Python that can be used to perform an array of operations easily.

Conditional and Looping Statements

The first few hours of this book have introduced some basic data types and possible operations. Now, let us get into what we call logical statements. The next set of syntaxes/statements that we need to learn are what we call conditional statements, which help take action based on the validity of a given condition.

Some of the commonly used conditional statements are

- If....else

- For loop

- While loop

- Break and Continue

Let us look at this syntax and examples using each of these conditional statements.

If...else

This is the basic conditional statement that instructs the interpreter to take action, defined within the 'if' block only when the given condition is true, and if not, the statements within the 'else' block are executed.

The syntax is;

if cond:

action1

else:

action2

For example, create a.py with the following statements:

if 5>2:

print 'true'

else:

print 'false'

Note the indentation used to define the if and else blocks, save the file as "cond.py" and execute the file as follows,

>>>python cond.py

True

Assume the condition was changed to

if 5<2:

print 'true'

else:

print 'false'

After executing the file, making the change and saving the same, the output will be,

>>>python cond.py

false

Some More Examples

>>>>if a<b:

>>>>pass #Does nothing

>>>>else

>>>>print "else case"

If you have to check more than one case, use the "elif" keyword to achieve the same as follows,

>>>>if a == '+' :

>>>>#Perform Addition

>>>>>elif a == '- ':

>>>>#perform subtraction

>>>>>else

>>>>#print unknown operator

For Loop

The 'for loop' is a conditional statement which iterates through the list/dictionary/tuple objects if the condition is still true. This conditional statement works both on user-refined or pre-refined data types.

The syntax is:

for var in list:

 action

For example: Let us declare a string and iterate through the characters,

>>> for var in str:

... print str

...

hello

hello

hello

hello

hello

The above for "loop", iterate through the string and prints the string for the number of times equal to the length of the string, by simply changing what gets printed one can see a different output – say each character can be printed as well.

>>> for var in str:

... print var

...

h

e

l

l

o

This syntax can be used to iterate over lists, dictionaries, and tuples to achieve the desired output.

While Loop

while <condition>

<action1>

else:

<action2>

This statement is used to make the interpreter keep repeating a specific action while a given condition is true. Therefore, as long as the "condition" is true, action1 is repeated, whereas when it returns as false, action2 in the else block is executed.

Pass Statement

This is a Python-specific statement, which can be used when a statement is required to be present in a given program for a syntactic reason, but not required to take any action. It instructs the interpreter not to do anything.

For example
def func1():
  Pass

Def Statement

The "def" keyword used in the above example is used to instruct the interpreter of the beginning of a definition of a function or method, with a function being a collection of statements used to achieve a specific action.

Break and Continue Statements

These two are other popular Python keywords, which can be used to control the flow of the program, and they simply perform what each word literally means.

Break – stops execution and breaks out of the loop/action that the program is currently in.

Continue – instructs the interpreter to continue performing the action in the block.

Advanced-Data Types

What makes python truly powerful is some of the inbuilt data types that it comes bundled with such as lists, dictionaries, and tuples. They are powerful as they enable us to undergo a wide variety of complex operations in the simplest possible way. Let us now look at how to best use these powerhouses.

Lists

Lists are nothing but a data type representing a one-dimensional array in Python, which can contain values of any other basic data types like numbers or strings.

Lists are one of the most powerful data types available in Python; they are dynamic, mutable and compatible with most of the other object types available in python.

Lists are enclosed by square brackets [] and each item in the list is separated with the help of commas.

For example,

```
>>>a = [1, 2, 3, 4, 5] # list of integer numbers.
>>>strList = [ "Sunday" , "Monday" , "Tuesday" ,
 "Wednesday" , "Thursday" , "Friday" , "Saturday" ]
# a list of strings.
```

There are several inbuilt operations possible on these list-objects such as

>>>*len(a)*

5

>>>*strList.reverse()*

["Saturday" , "Friday" , "Thursday" , "Wednesday" , "Tuesday" , "Monday" , "Sunday"]

The list can be easily sorted, while new elements can be appended or sliced and so many of these types of operations can be easily performed in a single statement. Some of the commonly used operations on lists are as follows:

>>> *sorted(strList)*

['Friday', 'Monday', 'Saturday', 'Sunday', 'Thursday', 'Tuesday', 'Wednesday']

Easily append an element to the list using the following method

>>> *strList.append('noDay')*

>>> *print strList*

['Sunday', 'Monday', 'Tuesday', 'Wednesday', 'Thursday', 'Friday', 'Saturday', 'noDay']

One can also use the '+' operator to concatenate two lists or add an element to the list, however, please note that the lists should carry elements of the same datatype. For example, we cannot concatenate strList and a, and this will throw an incompatible type error.

Other common operations include insert, delete, pop, remove, in, count, iteration, etc.

```
>>> a = [1,2,3,4,5]
>>> a.insert(0,0)
>>> print a
[0, 1, 2, 3, 4, 5]
```

Now, we can now remove an element from the list by using the index of the location.

```
>>> a.remove(0)
>>> print a
[1, 2, 3, 4, 5]
```

Dictionary

A dictionary object represents a hash table as a collection of key-value pairs. The dictionary is also a builtin data type, with the difference between a list and dictionary being that the former is an organized array while the latter is an unorganized collection, which means the values are not accessed using indices but by using the 'key' value. However, like lists, dictionaries are dynamic and can be of variable length.

Declaration:

dict1 = {key1:value1, key2:value2, key3:value3.... }

The dictionary elements are enclosed with flower brackets, with each key-value pair separated by a colon and with the pairs separated by commas.

Just like lists, tuples can be concatenated, repeated, sliced, indexed, iterated and length found, but operations like insert/delete are not possible as tuples are immutable.

However, it is possible to concatenate two tuples and save it in a third tuple, like the following

>>> tup2 = ("Hello","World", 2000, 1990)
>>> tup1 = (1,2,3,4,5)
>>> tup3 = tup1 + tup2
>>> print tup3
(1, 2, 3, 4, 5, 'Hello', 'World', 2000, 1990)

Some built-in functions, which can be used on tuples, include comparing two tuples and finding the min, max in elements of the tuple:

> > > *print tup1*
(1, 2, 3, 4, 5)
> > > *max(tup1)*
5
> > > *min(tup1)*
1

The compare method returns the value 0 if the tuples match and -1 if they do not:

> > > *print tup1*
(1, 2, 3, 4, 5)
> > > *print tup4*
(1, 2, 3, 4, 5)
> > > *cmp(tup1,tup4)*
0
> > > *print tup2*
('Hello', 'World', 2000, 1990)

>>> cmp(tup1,tup2)

-1

You can also convert a list to a tuple using the following function

>>> print a

[1, 2, 3, 4, 5]

>>> tuple(a)

(1, 2, 3, 4, 5)

Before we wrap up this chapter, let us look at one final example using the inbuilt enumerate function:

>>>>children = ['pop' , 'Beth', 'Charles', 'Kate']
>>>>for i, name in enumerate(children):
 >>>>print "iteration {iteration} is {name}".format
(iteration=i, name=name)

We have now looked at the commonly used dataTypes and possible basic operations on these data type objects.

Object-Oriented Programming with Python

As we now know, the Python language is object-oriented, with the programs structured into classes and objects, which are instances of classes that encapsulate data and methods that operate on these data.

A sample Python program using class and function can be defined using the following syntax:

import module
class MyClass:
#comments, variable declaration
def func1():
#function definition
def func2():
#function definition

The first statement is used to "import" modules/packages that contain pre-defined functions, which can be used in our program.

The keyword "class" is used to notify the interpreter that this is the beginning of the class definition. Each class will contain a variable declaration that can be accessed via the objects/methods of the class. The methods/functions that can operate on these class variables are defined using the keyword "def" . A function is nothing but a block of organized code that performs a specific action, and this block can be reused several times. A function can take arguments as inputs and the "return" statement is used to exit/return from the block. The scope of variables declared within the function is local to that specific function.

An object of a given class can be declared using the following syntax,

Obj1 = MyClass(args)

Args are the arguments that can be passed to the constructor of the class, and by default, all classes by default have a constructor with the name __init__(self)

The obj1 can then be used to access the functions defined using the "." as follows:

Sample Code

Obj1.func1()

Sample Program:

class Employee:

#Variable Declaration

empNo = 0;

def __init__(self, fname, lname):

self.fname = fname #first name of employee

self.lname = lname #last name of employee

Employee.empNo += 1 #employee count

def dispName(self):

print self.fname+self.lname #concatenated first and last name and prints that

emp1 = Employee("John ", "Bean") # creates an employee object

emp2 = Employee("Anne", "Hathway") #creates another employee object

emp1.dispName() #calls function using. operator to display name

emp2.dispName()

print "Total Count: %d" %Employee.empNo #prints count

Save the above code in a file, say sample1.py and executing the same will print the following output

>>>python sample1.py

John Bean

2

The above is a very simple example of writing a Python program using classes – basically, we concatenated the first and last name of the employees and printed the output to the console.

The first function defined in the class __init__() is called a constructor, and it is used to initialize objects. The statements

emp1 = Employee("" ," ")

Create an object with the respective values. In the above, note that a keyword "self" is passed as an argument to the functions. This is just a python convention; whether one uses this or not, this will not change the functioning of a given program, as it is used for readability of the code.

The functions of a class can be accessed either by using the "." operator or simply using the parentheses.

Importing and Using Modules

One of the most important and powerful aspects of Python is the inbuilt libraries/ modules which contain inbuilt functions that can be used in our programming. Through the course of the book, when we discussed program structure, we briefly looked at an introduction of the use of modules, with the statement used to import libraries being "import" .

A module is a logical way to organize Python code. The import statement can be used to import multiple modules at once simply by separating each module using a comma as follows,

>>>>*import module1, module2,...module*

To use a function belonging to a particular imported module, for example, func1 belonging to module1 needs to be used, like the following:

>>>>*import module1*

>>>>*module1.func1()*

With respect to using modules, another important keyword is "from" , as it enables the import of specific attributes from a module as follows:

>>>>*from module1 import func1*

The * which is called the wildcard character can be used to import all attributes belonging to a module.

The modules come bundled, as part of your Python installation and the interpreter knows to look up the modules. Generally, it first looks in the current directory and if unavailable, it goes through every directory under the path where Python is installed, all the way to the root /use/local/lib/python path. If still unavailable to find the modules, an error will appear asking you to install the specific library.

Using Files

Like for other high-level languages, files are another useful concept that Python supports. Apart from reading input from files and writing output to files, Python offers some useful hacks to work with files and directories that can be very handy when trying to write automated scripts on the file systems.

To open/create a file

Sample Code

>>>>f = open("file1.txt") #returns a file object

>>>>line=f.readline() #read line by line from the file

>>>>while line: # till eof

>>>>print line #print the line

>>>> line=f.readline() #read line by line from the file

>>>>f.close() #close the file object

The while loop can be replaced using a for loop and the same result can be achieved.

The open() API can take two parameters, the first being the file name and the second the parameter to indicate the permission mode in which the file is opened – to read, write and execute.

For example, to write to a file, it needs to be opened with write permission as follows

Sample Code

>>>>f.open("file1.txt" ,w)

>>>>f.write("hello!") #this writes the word "hello" to the file by name file1.txt.

>>>>f.write("Python is a fantastic language to use.\ extremely easy for beginners to learn.\n")

>>>>f.close()

Now if the file is opened, it will look like below,

hello! Python is a fantastic language to use.

Extremely easy for beginners to learn.

Note that the line starting with "extremely.." is printed in the second line - this is due to the newline format "escape sequence" used while writing to the file – '\n' . There are several such escape sequences (a character preceded by \) defined in the language which can be used to format how the output appears in a file or any other standard output.

Other common operations that can be performed on the file object are the following:

Operation	Description
f.closed()	Returns a Boolean: true if the file is closed, or false if it isn' t
f.mode()	Returns the access mode with which the file has been opened – it will either say read or write, etc
f.name()	This method returns the name of the file object.
f.tell()	Used to tell the current position of the pointer in the file
f.seek(x,y)	Used to move the pointer to a required position defined by the x, y position

In addition, predefined functions available in the "os" module such as renaming and deleting files can be used on os objects. In addition, Python provides several API to achieve common file operations provided by Linux commands such as mkdir to create a new directory or chdir to change directory path, etc.

For example:

import os #imports the os module

os.getcwd(); # gives the current working directory

Knowing how to effectively use files helps in writing many Python scripts useful to any programmer every day.

Error Handling, Debugging, and Documentation

This is a very important aspect of learning to program, as it entails how to spot errors, debug them efficiently, and quickly solve them. Errors can be either syntactical or logical and depending on that, they could be caught at different stages – either during runtime based on user input or simply due to the program failing to launch.

If we anticipate errors or wish to capture error cases, either for unit testing or for a specific use case, the following statements can be extremely useful.

The statements that can be useful while writing Python programs are the following.

Exceptions: try/except/finally – these are used together as blocks for error handling.

Assertions – assert to do a sanity check to test your program.

try:

 action ()

except:

 print 'action error'

else:

 #do this if no exception

A single try block can have multiple 'except' statements.

The keyword "raise" or "raise-if" can be used to explicitly throw an error, assert if the statement is true or not and verify the programs.

Apart from the inbuilt interactive interpreter, the ipython tool can also be used to learn and debug Python code. Another useful tool to have in the developer' s repository is pdb, a line-by-line debugger similar to gdb for C/C++ - is.

Decorators and other miscellaneous Python things:

Over the past 20 odd hours, we have looked at several fundamental python concepts as well as some basic programming techniques. In this chapter, we will focus on introducing some features unique to Python such as the decorator, which is used to redefine how a method behaves.

Any method or function preceded by an "@" symbol denotes the presence of a decorator.

Working with Time:

Python provides the following method to work with date and time - the module containing the necessary functions is "time" .

>>>>localTime = time.localtime(time.time()) #this statement will give the current time

Other modules associated with time manipulation are "calendar" , "dateTime" and "dateUtil" .

format	Python
seconds since the "Epoch"	time.time()
tuple	time.gmtime()
string	time.ctime()

Install Packages required for Machine Learning Applications

Before beginning any machine learning exercise, there are some essential packages to install which we have mentioned below. As we saw earlier, these packages contain various functions and features that will be used at different points when building machine learning models and systems.

Open a terminal and run the following commands

pip install numpy

pip install scipy

pip install SciKit-learn

pip install matplotlib

pip install pandas

Chapter 5: Data Scrubbing and Preparation

When building machine learning systems, one of the first steps to understand is how we collect the data sets that will be used to train the model, and how to take care of the scrub and clean it before feeding it to the system.

The dataset is normally prepared to depend on the application of the system - as a beginner-learning machine learning, there are several sample data sets available online that can be downloaded and used for experimenting and learning purposes, like the Iris data set, Real Estate and Stock Market data sets. Collecting data for new, specific applications are out of the scope of this book. Instead, we will look at how to prepare data using some examples in the subsequent sections.

Normally, this data is generated from real-life transactions and is, therefore, more likely to contain faulty entries, missing records or noisy data. A combination of such faulty data could then lead to a case of data contradiction - where the data in the data set itself are in contradiction with each other and end up confusing the model.

Here are some of the errors in datasets and how to scrub them.

Noisy Data

In real life, datasets are primarily generated based on signals from various sensors and other hardware devices. When the data is being collected, either due to hardware limitations or due to minor errors in hardware calibrations, there could be "noise" in the data collected. This unwanted data called noise could, in turn, affect the accuracy of machine learning models' outputs.

A common example of noise is when recording sound; the background noise is unnecessary data that is collected. Another example is when a classification algorithm is trying to classify the photos in a phone library based on image recognition of subjects in the photo; the unnecessary objects in the background have to be eliminated as noise in order for the algorithm to efficiently recognize and classify the photos.

There are several methods used to correct or minimize this noise such as Binning, Clustering, etc.

Binning Models achieve this by simply sorting the data and smoothing it based on neighboring data. This is called local data smoothing.

Clustering is particularly useful in eliminating outliers. Let us look at an example of how to understand the concept of outliers.

Assuming the system/machine learning model is a French person who is planning to travel to the United States. The model, therefore, needs to be trained to speak and understand English. When trying to train in English, which you have no prior knowledge of; you might believe that the best way to learn it is to learn every word of the legendary poet Shakespeare, as you have learned that he is one of the greatest poets that ever lived.

However, upon landing in New York and testing the model, we soon come to realize that the "Shakespearean English" is not understood, and we are not able to respond to the locals despite them also speaking "English". This is because we have been training with an utterly irrelevant extreme data set and the model has not been flexible enough to adapt to new training data.

This is a classic example of an overfit model, which has a high variance and low bias and therefore has poor generalization for new training data.

To rephrase this, the "model" we want is something that we can communicate using the "English" Language.

The "training data" are works of Shakespeare, but our "testing set" is New York.

If the model's performance is tested on "social acceptance", we see that the model fails on grounds of "generalization".

With such a model as context, one can understand "Variance" as the amount a model can change in response to the training data given. Our model is said to have "high variance" because it is highly dependent on the "training data". Therefore, it can be understood that any model with high variance will perform poorly when used with a new testing set.

On the other hand, bias is the exact polar opposite of variance; it is a measure of the strength of the assumptions we make about the data set. In our case, we completely trusted Shakespeare and this is a case of "low bias". Ideally, one should be skeptical about the data set and not have any assumptions that are not duly backed with reason.

This case of "low bias and high variance" is termed as "overfitted model". Therefore, in summary, any model should have a balanced tradeoff between bias and variance. Bias is a measure of our data strength and variance is a measure of the model itself.

Let us now look at what happens when the equation is reversed to "High Bias and Low Variance" . Such a model is called an "under the fitted model" , basically one that undermines the lessons from the training data set and fails to understand the relationship between input and output, thus resulting in failed results.

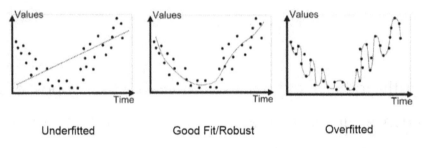

Underfitted   Good Fit/Robust   Overfitted

Image: Graph showing under fitted vs over fitted Model.

Let us apply this to our "English learning" example.
Say we make a few assumptions about our data and swap the training data set from Shakespeare to a popular US-based series, say, "House of Cards" to learn English. From experience, we know that the model is trained to

pick sentences that are in a particular format only - say, starting with an article and overlooking all other sentences. Having trained with this improved model, going back to the streets of New York, although the outcome is slightly better, the conversations are not exactly meant as we have not made an effort to understand the simple fundamental structure of the language. This is owing to our high bias regarding our training data.

This is a watered-down example of the concept of overfitting and underfitting models, and the bias and variance issues are addressed using various methods such as "data cross-validation", where the training data is split into subgroups and cross-validated several times.

In summary

- Overfitting: is the model that relies too much on training data

- Underfitting: is the model that fails to understand the underlying relationship in the training dataset

- High Bias: is the case where our assumptions lead us to ignore the factors of the training data

- High variance: is the case where the model' s response is directly and significantly affected by even the slightest change in training data.

Both overfitting and underfitting result in poor generalization, so to overcome these limitations, a validation set should be used to tune models.

Missing Data

After noisy data, the second most common issue with data sets is the case of missing data. Data sets are normally fed to the model in the form of tuples that are essentially a set of feature and attribute data.

Normally, if a particular tuple, the record has a lot of missing data against attributes; it is considered useless data or "Missing data" . One way to address this is to scan and "Ignore" all these tuples with unusual data attributes. However, this is not the most efficient way to address missing data.

An alternate approach to this is to find such missing data tuples and manually fill in the missing values. Although this will ensure higher accuracy, it is not a viable solution when working with enormous volumes of data as it is a time consuming, tedious and inefficient process.

A slightly more sophisticated solution is to predict the missing values of attributes by computing the available data and using it. This could be used to check and compare results obtained using the first method of ignoring tuples, however, this could cause a bias in data because predictions are not always accurate and this could lead to differences.

The next best option is drawing inference-based algorithms – some common algorithms used to infer and fill a missing value with the most probable value are the Bayesian formula and decision trees.

Inconsistent Data / Eliminating Duplicates

Another common cause of data discrepancy is the case of duplicates, which happens when some tuples and values are repeated causing inconsistencies, some of which can be corrected manually. In addition, there are specific tools available in the market to detect and correct this anomaly. A classic dataset that faces the issue of duplication is a patient record management system in hospitals, as the same patients enter data multiple times with different attributes on different visits.

Let us now look at an example and see how we can practically handle the missing data menace when building machine-learning systems.

The reason this is crucial is that most of the common statistical models aka algorithms will not proceed with processing the input data sets unless they are complete, with no loss or missed variables.

It is therefore imperative that the first step is to either eliminate such missing data or fill the missing data with estimated values as indicated in the previous section.

The first step is to determine if it is really a case of missing data, and the second is to identify if the source of data is responsible for consistently missing the value of the attribute. It could be missing either because it was forgotten or because it is irrelevant and was intentionally ignored at the source.

Here we will see how to use Python to fix the case of missing data. The sample dataset we have chosen to illustrate this is a real estate dataset – please head to Google to download the Sacramento real estate case study.csv file.

In this example, we will look at how to mark and delete incomplete records and how to find the average value, use it to estimate the approximate value for missing attributes and fill in the nearest value.

Step 1: First download the dataset and analyze it in order to understand it; the csv file will have close to a thousand records and eleven fields such as street name, city, sale date, cost, etc.

To find the missing values, the following steps can be followed

Open Python Interpreter on the terminal, create a file and name it "RealEstate_MissingValue.py" for the Python script.

Then, place this.py file and the.csv file containing the dataset that needs to be processed in the same working folder.

Step 2: Identifying the above code will open the csv file, read the first 10 lines and print the following output from which one can understand the essential attributes. These cannot hold a null value, and based on this we can now add the following condition in the python script to check for null values in these fields and identify invalid data entries.

The second step is to mark the missing entries with the following piece of code.

Step 3: The next step is to replace these zeros with marks that will indicate the missing value when the algorithm traverses this dataset.

The common tag used to mark unavailable missing data is "NaN" , and the same thing can be achieved using the following inbuilt functions replace() and insnull().

All subsequent operations will know to ignore the data marked as " Null" .

Once the python script is executed, the output generated will contain the number of NaN; this value can be cross verified with the previous output which contained a number of zeros so that we can ensure all zeros have indeed been replaced with NaN.

Further validation can be carried out by choosing a different subset in the csv file, such as the following:

print(dataset.loc[60:80, [4,5,6,9]])

Step 4: Now that we have identified and marked fields with missing values, the next step is to clean the data set by removing this data from the database. The algorithms like LDA or Linear Discriminant Analysis Algorithm does not work if there are NaN in the dataset, and this throws an error like

" Unexpected EOF while parsing file"

To overcome this issue, the "dropna()" function available as part of the "panda" package can be used to eliminate these NaN records as follows:

from pandas import read_csv

import numpy

dataset = read_csv(RealEstate.csv, header=none)

#Mark zero values as missing or NaN

print ((dataset[[4,5,6,9]] == 0).replace(0,numpy.NaN))

#drop rows with missing values

dataset.dropna(inplace=True)

Step 5: Now that the dataset is cleared, the site has been significantly reduced, and in order to fill approximate values, the following steps can be done to address the missing value problem.

The random value selected from another record.

Use a constant value.

Mean or Mode value of the records.

Import values from other models.

The API that can be used is "fillna()" from the same panda package.

In the case of classification and regression algorithms, this step will not be essential. Some programming languages like k-nearest neighbor easily ignore dataset with missing values and can work around it.

Data Preparation

In the previous section, we looked at the first part of preparing a dataset, including scrubbing and cleaning the chosen dataset, the first pre-processing step, and now, the following steps need to be followed to get the data actually ready to use in the data model.

Data Integration

In most real-life scenarios, datasets are collected from multiple sources; therefore, the process required to integrate all of the data into a single usable consistent format is called data integration. A simple example of this is if you were collecting real estate data from across the world - the measurement units could be yards, sq. mt. and so on depending on the region, so for these to become usable in a single system, they need to be aligned to a single format. One of the common issues arising in these cases is the redundancy of data, and this can be overcome with a "Correlation Analysis". This will result in reliable, high-quality learning data sets that ensure a faster and more efficient training of the model.

Data Transformation

Sometimes, it is efficient to use data in a particular format, and the process of converting available data to a desirable format is called Data Transformation. This step converts data from one format or unit to another, say from a nonlinear format to a linear format so that data analysis becomes more efficient and more meaningful.

Some of the common transformation techniques are:

Aggregation: This technique is where two or more data values of a single attribute are aggregated into a single value, like a summary. An example of this is when categories can be combined under a single umbrella category.

Normalization: This is normally used to represent a group of data using a specific range; for example, when accordingly normalizing power signal values that fall in a particular range and scale. Choosing whether to normalize or not depends on the data one is dealing with.

Generalization: This technique can be thought of as the exact opposite of aggregation - in the sense that aggregation is about summarization whereas the idea here is to transform lower-level values to higher-level attributes, which is called "hierarchy climbing"

Attribute Construction: The next technique of transformation is particularly used when one needs to simply analyze new attributes that can be extracted from previously available attributes, thus constructing attributes with what was already available.

Cross-Validation Using K-Fold Technique

This step is a statistical step applied to sample data in order to check the validity of a machine learning system.

It is primarily used to evaluate and expect the kind of performance from the given Machine Learning model. The benefit of using such a method is to get a glimpse of performance using a small sample set of data and to determine how the Machine Learning model will behave for a similar or new set of data, which has not been previously used to train the model. This is one of the ways to evaluate the model.

One of the common validation techniques is the k-fold cross validation where a given segment of the dataset is divided into two subsets, the training data, and the testing data.

The data set is normally divided into approximately equal parts. The first portion is usually considered as the testing dataset, while the remaining k-1, the second part of the dataset is used as the training dataset. Out of three validation methods, this is the preferred one due to three key reasons – it is easy to implement, very easy to understand and its results have lower bias than other methods.

Generating Test Data Sets

Normally, when working on machine learning applications, users, particularly beginners use readily available data sets from the internet such as the Iris data set for clustering and testing their data models, while data scientists working on specific large-scale applications have their own sensors and hardware to collect original real-time data that will be used to train the model and let the model draw inferences based on it.

Alternatively, the other developer-friendly method that one needs to be familiar with as a beginner is how to generate one's own test data sets. These are randomized datasets created using the inbuilt library of Python, and these are extremely handy as a beginner at learning programming, as well as when looking for reliable data sets to clean and test systems.

The test dataset is small-batch data that will allow you to test a machine-learning algorithm, model or test harness. The advantage of such test datasets is that they have well-defined properties like linearity and non-linearity, thus allowing the user to explore various scenarios and the way the algorithm behaves in each one.

The library that python uses for this purpose is the very powerful machine learning suite - sci-kit learn library which comes armed with an array of functions to generate such samples based on configurable test problems for both classification and regression-based supervised learning models.

Here are some problems and how you can use them with pythons sci-kit learn library, such as how to generate linear regression prediction problems, binary classification prediction problems, and multi-class prediction classification problems.

Test Data Sets

One of the common problems beginners face in developing and implementing machine-learning algorithms is evaluating if they have implemented the models correctly. Unlike another classical programming, in machine learning, a said script or program will look like it is running normally despite bugs. However, when testing with real actual data, all the gaps become visible. In order to avoid such surprises in the testing stages, the data scientist/developer, or the user can diligently generate test datasets, which are small, yet complete datasets that allow you to test the algorithms to keep them test ready.

These test data sets are also extremely useful as a tool to understand the behavior of algorithms and how they respond to changes in data and to extreme parameters.

As mentioned earlier, the advantage of generating test datasets is that they are comprehensive and have a wide variety of properties, and some of the ideal properties good to have on any test dataset are the following:

- They are easy to generate and extremely quick.

- The test datasets contain both known or understood outcomes which are extremely useful to compare with predictions

- The data thus generated are stochastic in nature, in the sense that they allow for random variations of the same problem model every time they are generated

- Because the data sets are small, they are very easy to visualize and use.

- As it is only test data, it is not limited by any constraints, thus enabling the data set to be scaled up easily with trivial data augmentation.

- Sci kit learns library, which comes armed with an array of functions to generate such samples based on configurable test problems for both classification and regression-based supervised learning models.

- Classification model deals with the problem of assigning a label to observations.

The make_blobs() API is used to generate blobs in the Gaussian distribution. The user can control the count of blobs as well as the number of samples to generate and host other properties of the blob.

Binary Moons Classification Algorithm

This is a binary classification algorithm and it is called this way as the output is a swirl pattern and looks like two moons. This is a suitable model involving data sets with non-linear class boundaries.

Chapter 6: Constructing a Machine Learning Model with Python

Building a machine-learning model may not be a linear process; however, as seen earlier, there are a number of well-defined generic steps across any application, which are the following:

- Define the Problem.

- Prepare Data.

- Evaluate Algorithms.

- Improve Results.

- Present Results.

To be more specific, let us look at the typical steps involved in building a simple machine learning model using Python starting from loading a sample data set to have a predictive visualization.

Installing the Python and Scipy Platform

We have already seen how to install Python and other relevant libraries, as well as a simple script to check the version of pre-installed libraries such as SciPy, Numpy, etc.

Loading the dataset

In this step, any of the datasets can be used, and in this section, we will look at in what way to load and apply the very commonly used Iris dataset. For any beginner, the Iris dataset is a great place to start, as it is simple and has many resources online. Download the iris dataset here:

https://archive.ics.uci.edu/ml/datasets/Iris.

This is perhaps one of the most well-known databases in the pattern recognition space.

One can either directly load it from the UCI site, but here we are using the panda library to load the dataset with column names and in proper tabular data visualization format.

In case of network access issues, the data set can be downloaded as a .csv file from this location and stored on the local file system, allowing it to be loaded as well.

Summarizing the dataset

This step involves multiple sub-steps finding the dimension of data such as the number of rows and columns called instances and attributes respectively.

Sample Code

 # shape

print(dataset.shape)

The output should be (150,5) 150 instances with 5 attributes.

The next step is to peek into the data and to visualize the actual data that you are working with. For this purpose, the following piece of code is used, which displays the first twenty rows of data:

Visualizing the dataset

By now, we have a good idea about the data we will be working with, and the next step it to visualize and see the whole dataset. There are two types of visualization plots available; one is the Univariate type of plot, which helps data scientists better understand the attribute and the second type of visualization plot is the Multivariate plot, which basically allows the user to see the relationship between the attributes.

For Univariate plots, when looking at each attribute, we see that the visualization can be picked based on the type of data. The output generated will give us a better idea about the allocation of the input data.

If you wanted to create other visualizations, like a histogram, for example, the code would look something like this:

Sample Code

 # histograms

dataset.hist()

plt.show()

Looking at the generated graph, if you are familiar with basic maths, probability, and statistical models, you can see that two of the attribute values have a Gaussian distribution, which is a suitable inference to have.

This information can help us determine the choice of the machine-learning algorithm to choose.

The next visualization model is the Multivariate Plot, which can be used to determine the relationship between attributes.

Sample Code
 # scatter plot matrix
scatter_matrix(dataset)
plt.show()

This will generate a scatter plot to show the relationship between two attributes. The generated graph will indicate diagonal mapping indicating the presence of "high correlation", which is, therefore, a predictable relationship between the data points available in the Iris Data Set on which we have been carrying out all these experiments.

Evaluating some algorithms

This is the most crucial step, as we are going to choose the machine learning model on which we can use the data set. The choice of algorithm or model depends on all the inferences we have got from the previous data analysis steps.

Once we have identified a model, the next step is to generate a validation data set that can be used to determine whether the choice of our data model is the best one. Of course, we can subsequently utilize statistical methods to evaluate the precision of the model.

Validation data creation is nothing but hiding part of the data set from the model and then subsequently using it to test the model.

The next sub-step in the lead up to choosing the right algorithm is cross-validation of data, and in this example, we will use what is called the ten-step cross-validation algorithm - this will basically split the entire data set into ten parts and train on nine out of the ten parts while retaining one part for testing, and this keeps repeating on loop for all combination of test trail paths.

Sample Code
 # Test options and evaluation metric
seed = 7
scoring = 'accuracy'

The seed can be any random number. One can use the rand() function or other random number generators in Python to get a seed value. The "accuracy" here is a pre-built metric available in the SciPy library, but we can use any scoring variable of our choice. This particular variable called "accuracy" is basically a ratio of the number of correct prediction occasions compared to the total number of instances in the database, which is in turn multiplied with a hundred to give the accuracy as a percentage.

Building Models

One can pick up only by trial and error and lots of practice this skill. For now, we will try to choose the best model based on the information we have gathered from all the data analysis done so far such as the linear data, etc.

Some of the commonly known linear and non-linear classification models are logistical regression, LDA or linear discriminant Analysis, the Naive Bayes, KNN or K - nearest neighbor and finally the classic SVM or Support Vector Machine algorithms.

From the output data generated, one can see the K-Nearest neighbor algorithm leading the accuracy measure among all the other algorithms in the race.

Another interesting tool to know is how to visualize the output generated for easy inference and plot the output data in a graph, like a histogram.

It 's clearly visible that K-nearest neighbor has better accuracy than the others in the race.

The K nearest neighbor algorithm was discovered to be the most accurate model for our Iris data set, so the same can be chosen for the next and final step in building a machine-learning model with python, which will be used to make predictions.

The sample output generated using the KNN model implemented as above indicates an accuracy of .9 or ninety percent. The confusion matrix generated indicates the flaws made and the final classification report indicates the breakdown of accuracy in each class-specific data. The validation data set that we had saved can now be used to cross-check the accuracy of the model chosen.

Sample Output

0.9

[[7 0 0]

[0 11 1]

[0 2 9]]

precision recall f1-score support

Iris-setosa 1.00 1.00 1.00 7

Iris-versicolor 0.85 0.92 0.88 12

Iris-virginica 0.90 0.82 0.86 11

avg / total 0.90 0.90 0.90 30

Chapter 7: Supervised Algorithms Implementation

Regression is a supervised learning algorithm and in this model, when given an input, we get an output that is normally a numerical value. Our interest here is not to learn the class but the numeric function that best describes the data. The objective is then to use this model to generate estimations.

One of the most common and simplest models is the linear regression model. It is the preferred model to find a predictive function when we have a correlation coefficient that indicates data predicting upcoming events.

The function is typically used to create a scatter plot of data based on the given input, and this usually creates a straight line. This linear regression is also the preferred method to show the linear relationship between two variables.

It is like the common and simple mathematical formula to calculate the slope of a line.

Y = mx + c

This is a common and largely popular simple algebraic equation, which can also be used to explain the linear regression concept in machine learning. We have a variable that is dependent, a function of another variable, and another variable that is an independent variable.

The objective is therefore to find the function that will help us determine how two given variables are related. In a dataset, we are normally given a list of values in a row and column format that can then be filled as the X and Y-axis values.

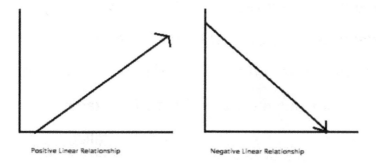

Positive Linear Relationship   Negative Linear Relationship

Image: Illustration to depict positive and negative linear regression

Linear regression or relationship is observing that when a single or more autonomous variable increases or decreases, the corresponding dependent variable also increases or decreases in tandem resulting in a slope as seen above.

As seen in the picture above, a linear relationship can thus be negative or positive.

Now, let us go back to the algebraic equation of a simple slope to understand how to implement regression models in Python.

We have seen that X and Y will have a relationship, however, in real life, this is not necessarily true. In the case of a Simple Linear regression on SLR, we will synthesize a model that is established by the data - the slope and the Y-axis infer from the data. In addition, we do not need the relationship between x and y to be exactly linear, as it could include errors in data, which are called residuals.

The objective is to simply take continuous data, find an equation that best fits the data and extrapolate and forecast or, in the future, predict a specific value. In the case of SLR or simple linear regression, we do exactly this by creating the best-fit line as shown in the scatter graph below.

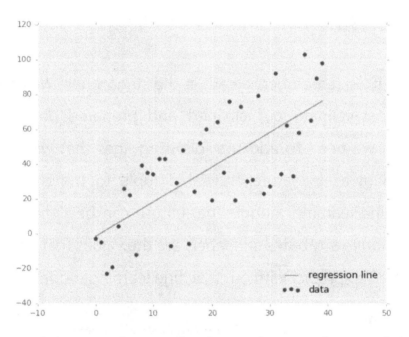

One of the popular applications of regression models is to predict stock prices or real estate market prices. Since regression is a form of supervised learning, the scientist trains the machine by exhibits it a set of features and corresponding correct answers repeatedly to train it to make predictions when a new input is given with similar features.

Remember the lesson from the previous chapter? Yes, the first step is to scrub, clean and prepare the data set. However, we can see that there are some redundancies and discrepancies in the pulled data set.

Now, if we remember, we are at the stage where we need to cross-validate our cleaned and prepared data, for which we need to add the following lines that will feed the data as a feature and label tuple to the classifier machine learning model. The feature can be defined as descriptive attributes and labels are the values that we are looking to predict with our machine learning models.

Classification Algorithm - Decision Trees

The objective is to make a design that forecasts the value of a target based on elementary decision rules that are implied from the data features.

In simple words, it is very similar to the common -if.. then.. else.. conditional statements that are commonly used as part of programming languages. This is more like a flow chart and it is a branch-based decision system. The algorithm is something that is very basic and easy to understand, like looking at an incoming email and classifying it as personal, work or spam based on certain predefined rules. This is as a very simple use case of decision trees.

A decision tree is literally a tree where one can take either route of the branches based on the answer to the conditional question at each node, with each branch representing a possible course action. Below is a simple decision tree example from real-life, where the tree can be used to determine whether a person is fit or unfit.

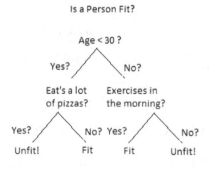

Image: A simple illustration of a Decision tree

Simple to understand and interpret and easy to visualize

This model requires little to no data preparation while other techniques require various steps such as normalizing the input data set, creating dummy variables, cleaning up blank or null values as well as scrubbing and reducing activity, which is not normally required. The use of this machine learning model significantly reduces the time and cost of execution. However, it is important to remember that this model requires missing data to be filled up, or else will it will throw an error and will not be able to proceed with further computation.

The number of data points determines the cost of execution, and the relationship of cost to the number of data is logarithmic to train the data model.

The other unique strength of this data model is that it works well with both numerical as categorical data, while several other approaches are usually specially designed to work with one format of data or the other.

Ability to employ multi-output problems

The white box model says that if any solution is observable in a model, the explanation for this condition can be easily explained using a Boolean logic equation. However, in the case of algorithms based on a black-box model like a synthetic neural network, the outcome could be tough to understand.

The other advantage is the ability to evaluate the model by using statistical trials, which makes the model more reliable than others do.

This model also performs well if the assumption is that datasets are slightly violated when applying the actual model, which ensures flexibility and accurate results irrespective of variance.

Some of the detriment of using decision trees involves:

1. Decision trees can generate overly complex trees that may not generalize data properly with the problem of overfitting. This can be overcome using techniques like pruning (literally like pruning the branch of a tree, but it is currently not supported in

Python libraries) - the task is to set up a few samples needed at a leaf node or setting the highest depth a tree can grow to, thus limiting the problem of overfitting.

2. The trees become erratic because of small variations in the input data, resulting in an entirely deviating tree generated. This issue can be overcome by using a decision tree within an ensemble.

3. NP-Complete problem - a very common theoretical computer science problem can be a hindrance in the attempt to design the most optimal decision tree because, under several aspects, the optimality can become affected. As a result, heuristic algorithms such as greedy algorithms with local optimal decisions at each node may become an issue. Teaching multiple trees to a collaborative learner can again reduce the effect of this issue and the feature and samples can randomly be sampled with replacements.

4. Concepts such as XOR, parity or multiplexer issues can be difficult to compute and express with decision trees.

5. In the case of domination of classes, the tree learners end up creating biased learners. Hence, it is important to adjust the data set before fitting it with the decision tree.

6. It is important to be conscious that decision trees gravitate to overfit data with plenty of features, and it is important to get the right sample and number of features in order for it not to become too highly dimensional.

7. Decision trees are extensively used in designing intelligent home automation systems - say, if the current temperature, humidity, and other factors are at a certain level, they can control the home cooling system temperature accordingly. Type systems are largely designed based on decision trees; something as simple as someone deciding to go out and play a game of golf can be considered a

series of decisions and can be modeled around a decision tree.

There are two key factors

- Entropy - the measure of randomness or impurity of the sample set - this must below!

- Information Gain – which is also called entropy reduction is the scope of the amount entropy has changed after splitting the dataset - the value of this must be high.

Chapter 8: Unsupervised Learning Algorithms Clustering

In the previous section, we saw various supervised learning algorithms such as the regression and classification algorithms, and in this section, we will look at two of the common unsupervised algorithms and how to model that using python.

As we have seen, the unsupervised algorithm attempts to create meaningful inferences from unlabeled data. Unlike the case of supervised learning, now there is no concept of target variable that we will be predicting. Instead, the objective here is to infer a description of the input data set given to us.

Simply put, in supervised learning, we were looking for an answer "y" based on the input data "x", however in unsupervised learning, we are looking to find what the model can say based on the given "x"

In the data science domain, we often think about how to use the data available to us to make predictions on new data points, which is "supervised learning." However, rather than 'making predictions', there are times when instead, we want to categorize the available data into categories. This is called "unsupervised learning."

Let's look at an example to understand this - say you are employed at a pizza outlet and have the task of creating a new feature for the order management software, which should be able to predict delivery times for customers based on historical data of previous deliveries, such as the distance traveled, the time that it took and other parameters such as the day of the week, time of the day etc. With this information, we can predict future delivery times.

Now, let us add a requirement to this - you are still employed at the same pizza outlet, but you are now tasked with segmenting your customers in order to run a targeted coupon campaign. Similarly, we have access to various historical data such as customer name, age, order, area, and other details. Classifying these customers into clusters like young, old and other factors is an example of "unsupervised learning", where we are not making predictions but merely categorizing the customers into various groups.

Real-Life Applications of Clustering

Some real-life applications of unsupervised learning include domains that deal with humongous and complex data sets such as genomics, to form clusters of genes with similar patterns. In addition, it is commonly used in astronomy, to classify different families of stars or celestial objects based on various factors such as their color, size, distance, materials, etc.

It is also extensively used to predict earthquake zones based on epicenter clusters, as well as in the following businesses:

- In driving targeted advertisements,

- In Netflix recommendations,

- Market segmentation,

- Image segmentation,

- Social media analysis,

- Image segmentation,

- Medical image detection,

- Anomaly detection,

- Recommendation engines,

- Search result grouping etc.

Classification of Clustering Algorithms

One of the two ways in which clustering algorithms are classified as on the means of which the input data is classified -

Hard Clustering: the kind of algorithms where the incoming input has to strictly belong to either one of the clusters - you either belong or do not - a case of binary classification.

Soft Clustering: this type of clustering algorithm is more pragmatic and more likely to happen in real-time applications of clustering because in most cases, the data tends to be in a grey area and does not necessarily belong to either one of the clusters. Therefore, unlike in hard clustering, the data here does not need to belong to one of the clusters. Instead, a value of probability is attached to indicate the likelihood of an input data belonging to one of the existing clusters. This way, we can predict if a customer is "more likely" to buy this and not come to an impractical conclusion saying the customer "will "buy this.

The classification of clustering algorithms include:

Hierarchical clustering

The second type of clustering algorithm is Hierarchical Clustering where the user does not define the k value; instead, the machine is allowed to decide on how many clusters should be created to cluster the data based on its own algorithms.

The other type of classifying clustering algorithms is based on the model of clustering - because the task of clustering itself is subjective, the following classification will throw light on the various approaches to clustering that are being followed.

Centroid Models

This relates to the class of clustering algorithms that are iterative in approach with the idea that similarity is derived based on how close a given data point is to the centroid of a cluster. The k means the algorithm is a classic example of this category of algorithms that are heavily dependent on the centroid. A user needs to predetermine and define the number of clusters thus making it remarkable to have past knowledge of a dataset that we are working with, which could be a limitation for certain applications that require to respond dynamically. The models run continuously to acquire the optimal central point.

Distribution Models

This classification works based on the probability of data points in an array falling under the same distribution class such as Gaussian or normal. These clustering models typically suffer from the issue of overfitting. A very popular algorithm that falls under this category is "Expectation maximization algorithm" which is used in the multivariate normal distribution based data.

Density Model

The data points from the input data set are plotted on to the graph, and they are more likely to vary in density across the data space. This variation in density is the basis of clustering for a few clustering algorithms which fall under the density model. These function by isolating various density regions and identifying sample data points from each and some popular models in this category are DBSCAN and OPTICS.

Implementation of Clustering Algorithms

In this book, we will explore two of the most common forms of clustering: k-means and hierarchical.

K-Means Clustering Algorithm

Clustering, which is sometimes called unsupervised classification, is one of the most popular algorithms; the k in the name refers to how many different unique clusters one wishes to generate from the given data set.

The user defines the value of k and each cluster formed has a centroid. The centroid is the central point of all the points that form any given cluster and the number of the centroid is equal to k - the number of clusters. This algorithm primarily works with numerical values and all other symbolic data types are excluded.

The major advantage and reason for the algorithms' popularity are how simple and easy it is to understand and implement as well as how quick it is in its execution.

The input data are automatically assigned into clusters and are therefore very beginner-friendly.

If we were to look at disadvantages or limitations of picking k means, its fact that, the k value has to be pre-entered before the beginning of execution thus limiting dynamic adjustments if required.

In addition, the output can be significantly influenced by the seed data that is initially fed to the model. The algorithm tends to converge to the local minimal and it is therefore recommended to reset and rerun the algorithm with different random seeds to ensure minimal error.

It is not most efficient when working with large data sets, and is therefore not scalable for large real-time applications. Sampling can at times help in making the runs quicker on large datasets.

The other major disadvantage is how sensitive the algorithm is to outliers, as a single outlier data could significantly alter the clustering efficiency of the model.

The mean value tends to be skewed if the input data set contains unusually large values (outliers), and a suggested solution to address this issue is to use the 'median' value instead of the 'mean'

Chapter 9: Deep learning with Tensor Flow

As we have seen, Deep learning is the core subset that defines the actual mathematical models that define the functions of machine learning systems and thereby drive artificial intelligence. In this chapter, we will briefly look at an introduction to the TensorFlow framework, which is Google' s largest python-based outline to create Deep Learning models.

Deep Learning systems can be defined as a category of machine learning designed to utilize advanced multi-layer neural networks. The concept of deep learning has been about since 1943 when Warren McCulloch, a neurophysiologist and Walter Pitts, a mathematician published a paper on how neurons should function, demonstrating a basic neural network with the help of electrical circuits.

Over the years, many, many developments have occurred and have enabled deep learning systems to become a reality. These mathematical models are extremely computationally costly and highly accurate, and with the recent advances in everything from the improved processing power of GPUs to the ever-increasing CPU power and network speeds to general computational capabilities, Deep Learning has become possible, leading to a sudden explosion of its popularity and becoming a hot topic in computing research.

TensorFlow was however created with the limitations of its processing power in mind. The framework, which was Open sourced in November 2015, has a library designed so efficiently that it can be run on computers with multiple computing abilities including smartphones. This allots for the immediate establishment of trained production models, and at the time of writing this book, it is currently the number one Deep Learning framework. It is extremely popular as it encapsulates all the complexities of deep learning functions and allows the user to focus on building the actual deep learning model.

Let us now look at how the tensor flow is designed and how deep learning applications are developed in this framework. In tensor flow, everything is created based on a computational graph. One can imagine computational graphs to be a chain of nodes, where every node (known as an operation) is running some computational function which can be as simple as an addition or a subtraction to as complex as multivariable mathematical equations.

The node or operation often referred to as "op" in the tensor flow parlance can return "zero" or more "tensors" which can, in turn, be used later on in the graph. The following are some examples of a sample list of operations and their corresponding output:

Each op or operation can be handled as a constant, an array, or a matrix (unit or n-dimensional matrix). The other word to refer to a multi-dimensional matrix (n-dimensional matrix) is the "tensor" . In other words, a two-dimensional tensor is identical to an m*m matrix.

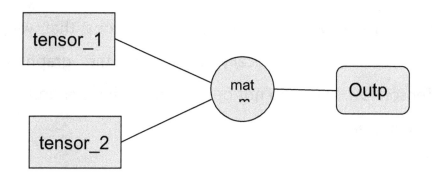

Image: Illustration of a sample computational graph in Tensor Flow

The above image shows a computational graph that depicts two tensors, including constant tensor nodes that are being multiplied to give the output. This is a very simple example to illustrate what a computation graph in Tensor Flow framework looks like. This is how one creates a graph to run a session; thus, one needs to understand that all inputs necessary by the tensor node or op are run automatically and mostly as parallel operations. When this graph session is running, it actually results in the execution of three operations: the creation of two constant tensor nodes and the operation of matrix multiplication.

Now, these two constants and operations that were created are automatically added to the graph in TensorFlow. These do not depend on each other and can still be created in one single file.

The next basic terminology or concept a beginner must be familiar with in the world of tensor Flow is the concept of "Sessions" . There are typically two types of sessions: tf.session() - This type of session happens when the environment in which the operations and tensors are evaluated and executed are encapsulated together. Sessions in tensor flow have their individual variables, queues, and readers given to them. Therefore, if one opens a session, one must also remember to close the session by using the "close()" method just like one would exit a thread in java.

Any session in a tensor flow framework typically takes three arguments, but all of the three are optional arguments.

Target - which refers to the choice of an execution engine that the current session must connect with

Config - a config proto procedure buffer with configuration options for the session.

Graph - The parameter that defines which computational graphs must be launched.

This function happens when all required dependencies needed for the graph to execute are invoked with one single function call.

The next type of session is tf.InteractiveSession() - which is used to achieve the same function as tf.session(), except it can be used for sessions using Ipython and Jupyter Notebook which allow the user to add things and use API like tensor.eval() and operation.run() alternatively of having to run the session.run() each time youhave something to be computed. Note that the user does not have to explicitly pass the session object in case of an Interactive session type function.

Variables

In the tensor flow framework, variables are managed by sessions and persist across sessions, which makes sense considering the operations and tensor objects are in fact immutable in the tensor flow framework.

The API used to create variables is tf.Variable()

Some rules to remember while creating variables in the tensor flow framework are the following.

Scope

In tensor flow, Scope is the term referring to the concept that defines the complexity of the computational graph. It is primarily used to break down tensor flow models in smaller pieces on the tensor board into individual pieces, thus controlling the complexity of the model. The tensor flow framework also supports the nesting of scopes. The real use of scopes can be appreciated when working on complex systems only in collaboration with tensor boards.

Sample Code

with tf.name_scope("Scope1"):

with tf.name_scope("Scope_nested"):

nested_var = tf.mul(5, 5)

With these fundamental blocks of tensor flow, one can build complex computational models in Deep Learning.

There is certainly much more to the framework than these basic elements, but they are beyond the scope of this book. These building blocks can help to get started with Deep learning experiments in tensor flow and elicit curiosity to enable further reading in this space.

Chapter 10: Case study: Sentiment Analysis

One of the most popular and fascinating fields in the application of machine learning in recent times has to be the field of Sentiment Analysis – which relates to how much a user enjoyed a movie based on the analysis of a bunch of reviews or understanding the current mood of a user based on their social media status, which is used to offer relevant services, as well as in plenty other cases in business.

A very common application of such a classification model based sentiment analysis is seen in automated intelligent home solutions where applications that run on home gateways such as routers collect data from other WiFi connected devices and sensors which are part of the home automation kit - data such as if the light is on, the temperature in the room, the weather and the number of people in the house and this is used to learn the pattern of usage and preference of each user. This data collected can then be scrubbed, cleaned and loaded and probed to make various useful inferences, which can, in turn, be sold to service providers that can offer a variety of services. These range from maintaining ambient temperature in the house, to ensuring better energy efficiency by automatically maintaining electrical appliances, to taking stock items in the fridge, pantry and notifying the owners about the stock in the pantry, and maybe even going one step further for grocery lists by automatically placing orders at the nearest store to be delivered to you.

Other services that a lot of large companies are looking to include is how this data can be used to provide mental health services to inmates and with an increasing number of adults living alone, applying anomaly detection category algorithms to detect any variation in daily routine to offer timely service.

In this section, we will look at the sample code for a simple sentiment analysis program using Python.

To do this, the reader is encouraged to download a readymade dataset of choice from the Internet. In this example, a sample dump of a movie review was taken and preprocessed using a script. The data thus cleared of missing values is then converted using the following piece of code into a readable and usable format in Python.

Sample Code

```
reviews_train = []
for line in open('../data/movie_data/full_train.txt', 'r'):
    reviews_train.append (line.strip())
reviews_test = []
for line in open('../data/movie_data/full_test.txt', 'r'):
    reviews_test.append(line.strip())
```

The text file containing a dump of review dataset looks like this:

*"This isn't the comedic Robin Williams, nor is it the quirky/insane Robin Williams of recent thriller fame. This is a hybrid of the classic drama without over-dramatization, mixed with Robin's new love of the thriller. However, this is not a thriller, per se. This is more a mystery/suspense vehicle through which Williams attempts to locate a sick boy and his keeper.

Also starring Sandra Oh and Rory Culkin, this Suspense Drama plays pretty much like a news report until William's character gets close to achieving his goal.

I must say that I was highly entertained, though*

*this movie fails to teach, guide, inspect, or amuse. It felt more as if I was watching a person (Williams), as he was actually performing the actions, from a third-person perspective. In other words, it felt real, and I was able to subscribe to the premise of the story.

All in all, it is worth a watch, though it is definitely not Friday/Saturday night fare.

It rates a 7.7/10 from...

the Fiend:."*

For this data to be usable, the following script for regular expression processing can be used to eliminate space and extract the meaningful data required:

Sample Code

```
import re
REPLACE_NO_SPACE =
re.compile("(\.)|(\;)|(\:)|(\!)|(\ ')|(\?)|(\,)|(\ ")|(\()|(\))|(\[)|(\])")
REPLACE_WITH_SPACE =
re.compile("(<br\s*/> <br\s*/>)|(\-)|(\/)")
def preprocess_reviews(reviews):
 reviews = [REPLACE_NO_SPACE.sub("", line.lower()) for
line in reviews]
 reviews = [REPLACE_WITH_SPACE.sub(" ", line) for line in
```

reviews

return reviews

reviews_train_clean = preprocess_reviews(reviews_train)

reviews_test_clean = preprocess_reviews(reviews_test)

The next step in the process is to convert all this data into a machine-readable numeric format, which is called vectorization.

In the next step, we will look for the largest and smallest coefficients and thereby determine the 5 most discriminating words in a positive and negative review.

Sample Code

```
feature_to_coef = {
 word: coef for word, coef in zip(
 cv.get_feature_names(), final_model.coef_[0]
 )
}
for best_positive in sorted(
 feature_to_coef.items(),
 key=lambda x: x[1],
 reverse=True)[:5]:
 print (best_positive)
```

('excellent', 0.9288812418118644)
('perfect', 0.7934641227980576)
('great', 0.675040909917553)
('amazing', 0.6160398142631545)
('superb', 0.6063967799425831)

```
for best_negative in sorted(
feature_to_coef.items(),
key=lambda x: x[1])[:5]:
print (best_negative)
```

('worst', -1.367978497228895)
('waste', -1.1684451288279047)
('awful', -1.0277001734353677)
('poorly', -0.8748317895742782)
('boring', -0.8587249740682945)

This simple classifier will look for these words in the review and classify them as good or bad reviews. The ones with words such as worst, waste, awful, poorly, boring will be classified as negative reviews and the ones with words such as excellent, perfect, great, amazing, and superb will be classified as being positive reviews.

Conclusion

Thank you for making it through to the end of *Learn Python Programming*, let' s hope it was informative and able to provide you with all of the tools you need to achieve your goals whatever they may be.

We hope the content in the book was helpful in getting a head start to machine learning and programming in Python. The best way to continue learning is by practicing and writing more code, taking up simple problem statements and trying to solve them using the concepts learned and when that is not possible, trying to find a way to solve the problem using new/advanced concepts.

Explore more functions and features in the several inbuilt libraries such as SciPy, NumPy, PyRobotics and Graphical User Interface packages such as wxPython, which can be used to develop powerful applications.

To summarize, Python is a high-level object-oriented language, which is an interpreter -based, making it highly portable and extendable, and its inbuilt libraries support a variety of functions to support Graphical User Interface, working with databases, etc.

The language is strongly typed, and it supports several dynamic data types and automatic garbage collection and it can easily be integrated with other high-level language programs like C, C++, Java, etc, making it a great scripting language.

We' ve seen the basic design philosophy of Python, some useful tools like the interpreter and visualizer that can be used to learn the language, basic syntax of common Python statements, data Types and finally program structures using classes and objects.

Using these basic building blocks, the reader can further learn about more complex data types, operations on the data type objects, file operations, defining own data Types and functions and so on.

Machine Learning is becoming a ubiquitous computing concept and it is becoming more and more relevant and essential to understanding this paradigm, and hopefully, this book should have equipped you with the necessary tools and insights to start building simple machine learning applications.

By now, one would have understood that machine learning is not that black box with those undecipherable, complex terms nor is python as terrifying as its namesake reptile. We hope this book has given you the confidence to start programming and designing machine learning models of your own.

Thank you once again for taking the time to read the book, and it is now time to explore the world of Python and unleash the power of programming with what we have learned.

Finally, if you found this book useful in any way, a review on Amazon is always appreciated!

www.ingramcontent.com/pod-product-compliance
Lightning Source LLC
Chambersburg PA
CBHW071113050326
40690CB00008B/1210